Tiki Essentials

What every Smarty needs to know
about Tiki Wiki CMS Groupware

by Rick Sapir

Tiki Essentials:
What every Smarty needs to know about Tiki Wiki CMS Groupware

by Rick Sapir

ISBN: 978-0-557-76676-5

Table of Contents

CHAPTER 1

Welcome to Tiki Essentials

What every Smarty needs to know about Tiki Wiki CMS Groupware

In 2007, I created ***Tiki for ~~Dummies~~ Smarties: A beginner's guide to using Tiki Wiki CMS Groupware*** (a.k.a. Tiki Basics). **Smarties**, as it became known as, has been a highly useful resource for the Tiki Community. I've heard from people around the world, all expressing their appreciation. Of all the feedback I've received, the most common comment, after "thanks for making this guide available," has been:

OK, I've got my Tiki up and running. Now what?

To answer this question, I created this guide of "essential" (to me, anyway) information for all Tiki administrators: ***Tiki Essentials***. In it you'll find my tips and tricks on how to get the most out of Tiki (and how to give back and become involved with the Tiki Community). As with **Smarties**, this book does not cover everything there is to know about every Tiki feature; but ***Tiki Essentials*** will help you take your Tiki beyond the basics and into the next level!

IN THIS CHAPTER

About this guide

This guide is intended for both new and experienced Tiki administrators. Not only will this book help you improve your Tiki site, but you'll also learn how to get the most out of your participation in the Tiki Community. It will show you how to find what you're looking for and how to become more involved. There are many different ways to contribute to Tiki Wiki CMS Groupware.

Tiki Essentials guide is based on Tiki Version 6. Complete information about Tiki can be found at the Tiki Community portal: **http://tiki.org**.

DISCLAIMERS

This guide *is not* a replacement for the official Tiki Documentation. Instead, this guide will expand your knowledge of a few essential features. You should explore the Tiki documentation and community portal for complete information on everything that Tiki has to offer.

I make no guarantees as to the accuracy or completeness of any information presented here. By using this book, you agree to do so at your own risk. You further agree to not hold the author (Rick Sapir) liable for any results that may occur from the use of the products mentioned herein.

ABOUT THE TIKI ESSENTIALS WEBSITE

The Tiki Essentials website (http://twessentials.keycontent.org), from which the content of this guide was created, is a "living" document, continually updated. I encourage you to become a contributor by registering at **http://twessentials.keycontent.org**, a website with material beyond the scope of this guide.

What every Smarty needs to know about Tiki Wiki CMS Groupware
http://twessentials.keycontent.org

Using this guide

I have written this guide in straight-forward, easy-to-understand language. Anyone familiar with the Web and computer software should have no problems following along (even if new to Tiki).

This section includes some basic information that you should keep in mind as you work through this guide:

- conventions
- references
- images
- translations

CONVENTIONS

Throughout this guide, you will find tips, notes, and warnings.

Warning *This is how a warning appears. Pay close attention to each warning. There aren't many, but they are important. You could crash your Tiki or corrupt the database, making your site inaccessible.*

Tip *This is how a tip appears. Tips are helpful hints that will make your Tiki experience easier, such as providing alternate ways of accomplishing a task.*

Note *This is how a note appears. Notes are secondary information that you may need.*

REFERENCES

References to web sites are shown in **bold** type. Additionally, references to the official Tiki Community sites are identified with the Tiki icon These links contain detailed information and are *highly* recommended.

Items and options within the Tiki interface are also shown in **bold** type.

IMAGES

All images in this guide are taken from **Tiki 6** using the default **Fivealive** theme. Depending on your installation options, your screens may appear differently.

TRANSLATIONS

Tiki includes powerful multilingual tools. Translations of this guide into other languages are available at the *Tiki Essentials* website: **http://twessentials.keycontent.org**.

Legal information

COPYRIGHT

IMAGES

The screen images are from Tiki Wiki CMS Groupware Version 6, and are made available under the GNU Lesser General Public License, Version 2.1 (LGPL).

The cover image is by Flavio Takemoto (**http://www.takemoto.com.br**), and is used with permission.

NAMES AND TRADEMARKS

Tiki, Tiki Wiki CMS Groupware, and the Tiki logo are trademarks of the Tiki Software Community Association, used with permission. **Tiki Essentials** is unaffiliated with the Tiki Software Community Association.

Other product names mentioned in this guide may be trademarks or registered trademarks of their respective holders and are used herein for identification purposes only.

About the author

My name is **Rick Sapir**. I have been developing technical content for software and other industries for over 15 years.

I have been using Tiki for a variety of Web projects (including **KeyContent.org** and *Tiki for ~~Dummies~~ Smarties*) since early 2005. I originally choose Tiki as my CMS platform because of its large feature set. There are other applications for wikis, forums, blogs, and such, but none are as fully integrated as Tiki.

My first contributions to the Tiki project involved minor updates and tweaks. I steadily became more involved, contributing additional code to the Tiki repository, joining several Tiki teams, and producing my *Tiki for ~~Dummies~~ Smarties* guide. In 2009, I was named to the Tiki Admin Group (TAG), and later became a member of the Tiki Software Community Association.

I continue to be active in the Tiki community (using the handle **ricks99**) on the Tiki IRC channel (**#tikiwiki**), answering forum questions, tweeting away, and doing what I can to improve the Tiki community.

You can learn more about me at **http:/ricksapir.com.**

ACKNOWLEDGEMENTS

I am grateful to the following people for their assistance in producing *Tiki Essentials*:

- **Ronald W. Garrison** (http://home.roadrunner.com/~rwgarrison/) for his work in reviewing and editing this guide
- **luciash d' being** (http://twitter.com/luciash),

   Louis-Philippe Huberdeau (http://lphuberdeau.com), and

   Filipus Klutiero (http://tiki.org/UserPageChealer9), for their technical review of this guide
- **Flavio Takemoto** (http://www.takemoto.com.br) for his artwork which adorns the cover of this guide

Finally, I extend my utmost gratitude to the entire Tiki Community. Without the work of its thousands of members, there would be no Tiki for me to write about.

CHAPTER 2

Getting Started with Tiki Wiki CMS Groupware

Tiki is a community-based open source project. Community members continually add new features (and improve ones), fix bugs, and patch security holes. It is important that you are familiar with the information in this chapter in order to keep your Tiki up to date, especially for security purposes.

FIGURE 2.1   *The Tiki installer makes installations and upgrades easy.*

If you've already installed and configured your Tiki (possibly with the assistance of **Tiki for ~~Dummies~~ Smarties**), this chapter may be a review for you. However, it is always a good idea to review this information.

IN THIS CHAPTER

Installing Tiki

This section includes some "essential" installation information that all Tiki administrators should know, including:

- Creating the database
- Using the Tiki Installer
- Performing a manual installation

Tip *See ⚡ **http://doc.tiki.org/Requirements** to review the Tiki installation requirements. Your webhost may also provide Tiki installation via a control panel application such as Fantastico or SimpleScripts.*

CREATING THE DATABASE

When creating a new database for Tiki, be sure to set the database's collation and the MySQL connection collation correctly. Tiki uses **UTF-8** as the default database character set.

FIGURE 2.2 *Creating a new database with UTF-8 collation*

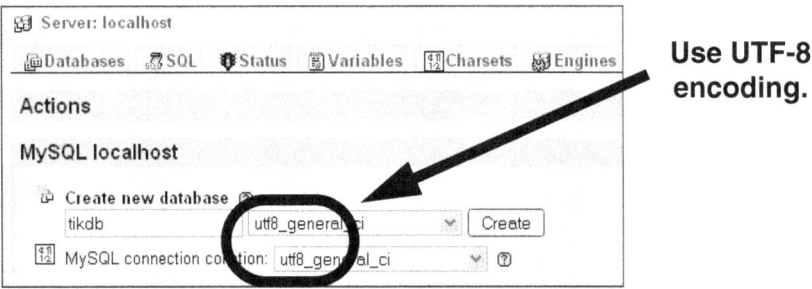

Note *In some hosted environments, you may not be able to specify the collation. In that case, contact your webhost for details on selecting the correct collation type.*

If Tiki detects that your database does not use the correct encoding, Tiki can attempt to convert your database to UTF-8.

FIGURE 2.3 *Tiki can attempt to fix your database.*

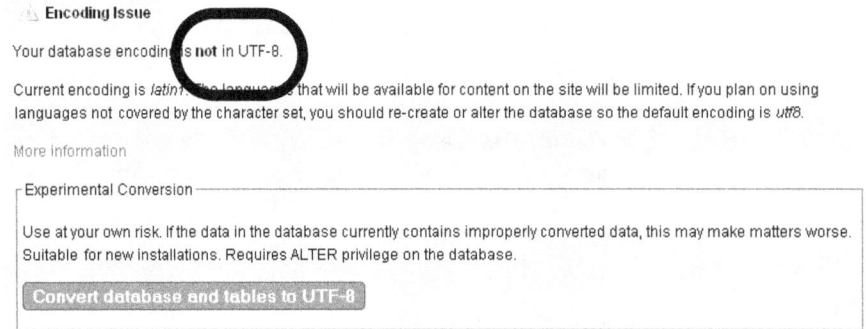

Warning *Be sure to back up your database before attempting the conversion.*

Database User

You will also need to create a database user with the following access to the database.

FIGURE 2.4 *Granting database user privileges*

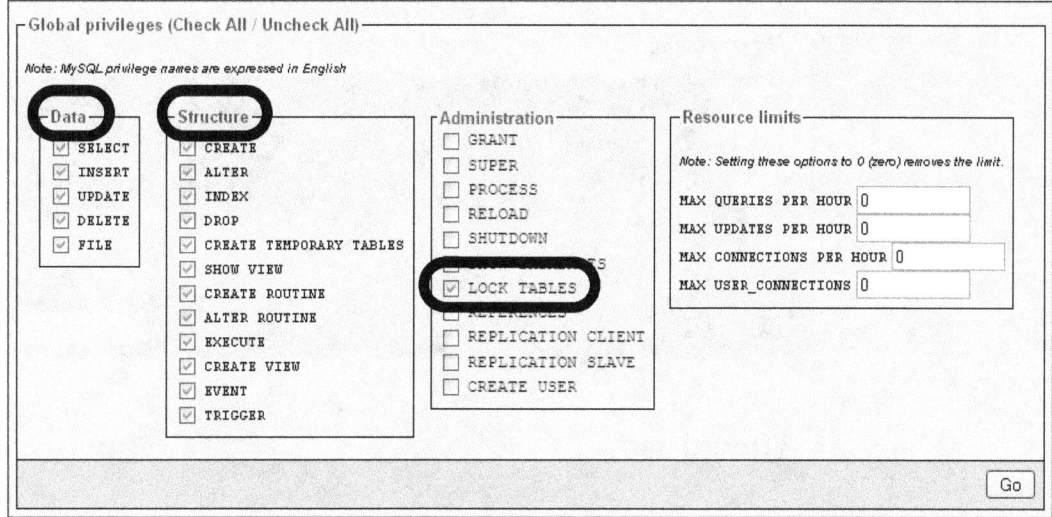

Note *Some webhosts will automatically create the database user when you create the database; creating a new database user may be unnecessary. Check with your provider for details.*

Be sure to record the following information, you will need it to complete the Tiki Installer:

- Database name
- Database user name
- Database user password

USING THE TIKI INSTALLER

The Tiki Installer features a wizard-like approach for installing Tiki Wiki CMS Groupware. Simply follow the prompts on each page of the installer!

To install Tiki:

1. Download Tiki by using the **Download** link on  **http://tiki.org**.

FIGURE 2.5 *Downloading Tiki*

The Tiki archive is hosted on SourceForge.net (an online resource for open source software development and distribution) and available in multiple formats, for different platforms.

Note *There are different versions of Tiki available, including the current Stable version and the Long Term Support (LTS) version. See* **http://dev.tiki.org/Version+Lifecycle** *for details.*

2. Upload (or unzip) the Tiki files to your host.
3. Open your web browser to: **http://*YOUR DOMAIN*/tiki-index.php**.

Note *If you are upgrading an existing site, you will need your database username and password to complete the **Tiki Installer Security** page and "unlock" the installer. See* **http://doc.tiki.org/Installation** *for details.*

4. On the **Welcome** page, select your language. The Tiki Installer reloads in your selected language. Click **Continue**.

FIGURE 2.6 *The Tiki Installer*

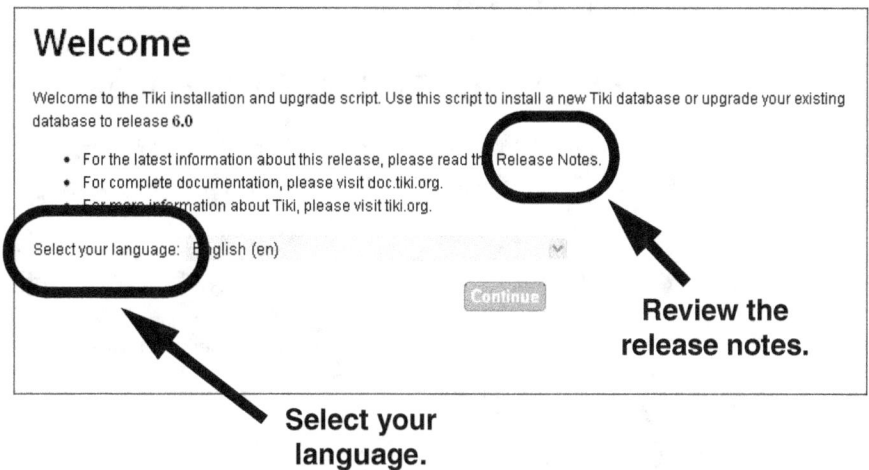

Select your language.

Review the release notes.

Note *The installer contains links to the release notes and documentation. You should review these for the latest information.*

5. On the **License** page, review the Tiki license and click **Continue**.

Tiki is available under the GNU Lesser General Public License (LGPL).

FIGURE 2.7 *Reading the license*

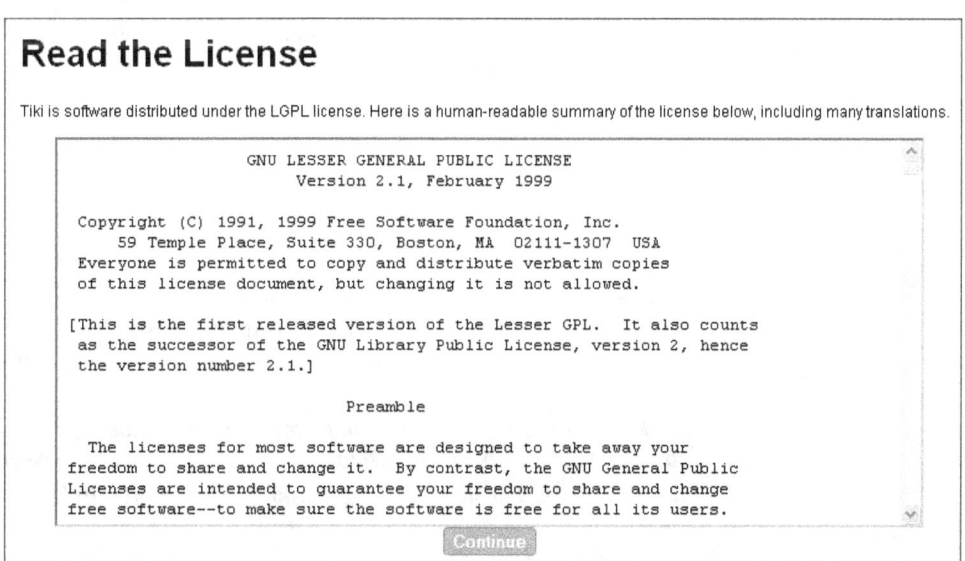

6. On the **Review the System Requirements** page, confirm that your system meets the minimum requirements and has the necessary image libraries. Click **Continue**.

FIGURE 2.8 *Reviewing the system requirements*

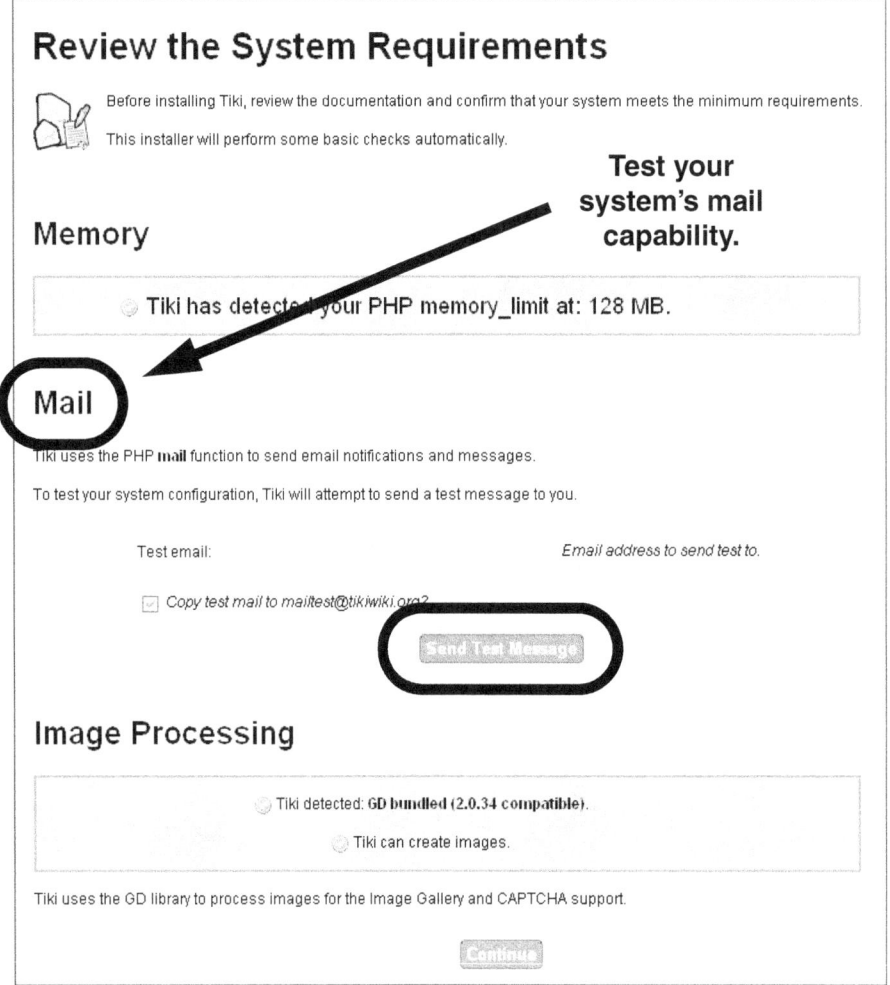

You can test your system's ability to send Tiki-generated mail messages by sending a test message. Enter your e-mail address and click **Send Test Message**. You should receive a sample message (sent from your new Tiki).

Note *By default, Tiki uses the PHP **mail** function to send messages. If your webserver configuration does not allow Tiki to use this function, you can use SMTP (Simple Mail Transfer Protocol) instead. See* **http://doc.tiki.org/smtp** *for details.*

7. On the **Set the Database Connection** page, enter your database information (see "Creating the database" on page 8) and click **Continue**.

Note *If you are performing an upgrade, Tiki will automatically detect the existing database connection information.*

FIGURE 2.9   *Setting the database connection*

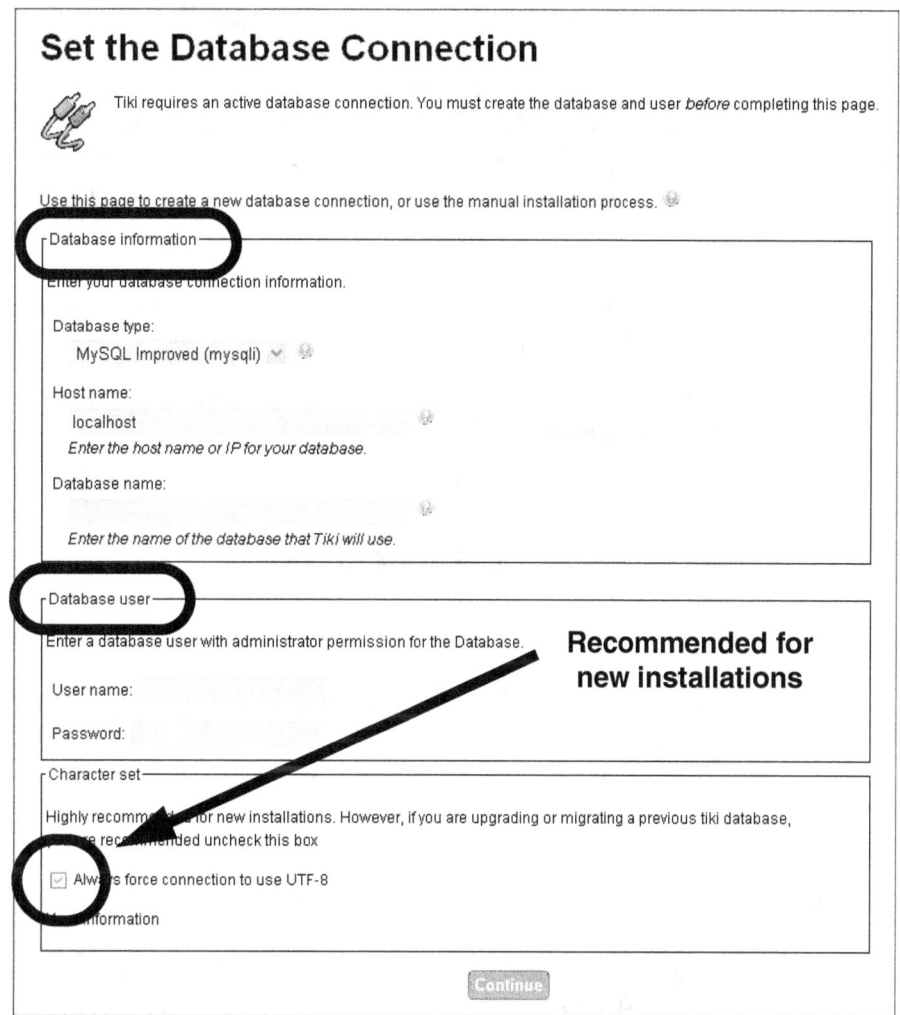

By default, Tiki uses UTF-8 for your database encoding. You should enable the **Always force connection...** option for UTF-8 databases.

See "Creating the database" on page 8 and "Performing a manual installation" on page 16 for more information on specifying database encoding.

8. On the **Install & Upgrade** page, click **Install**.

FIGURE 2.10 *Installing and upgrading Tiki*

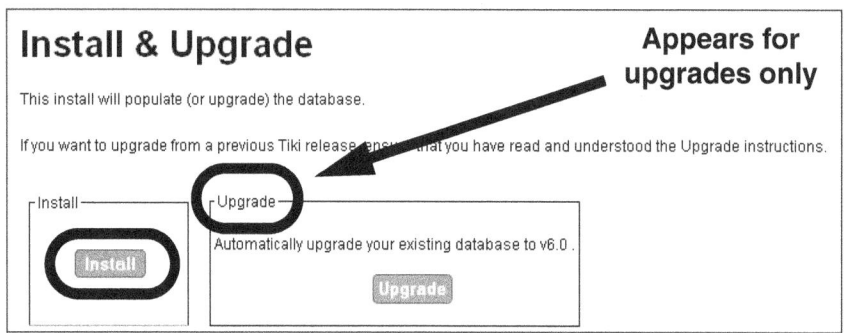

Note *If you are upgrading an existing site, click **Upgrade**. Always back up your Tiki files and database before upgrading. See "Backing up your Tiki" on page 22 for details.*

9. On the **Review the Installation** page, confirm that all queries were completed successfully and click **Continue**.

FIGURE 2.11 *Reviewing the installation*

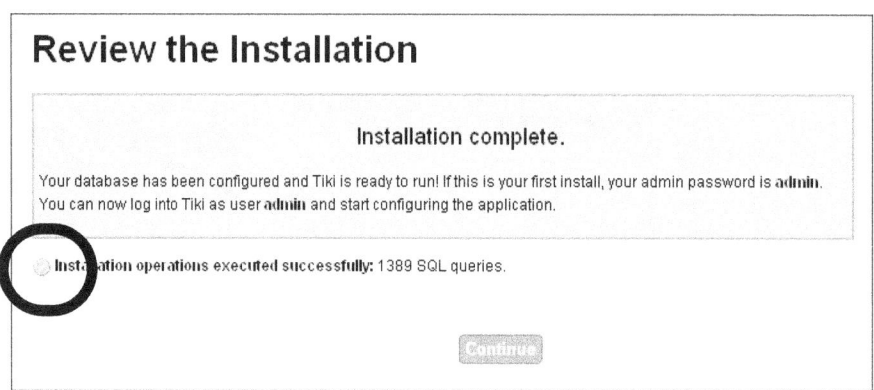

10. On the **Configure General Settings** page, enter the information for your site and click **Continue**. You can always edit or update this information later.

FIGURE 2.12 *Configuring general settings*

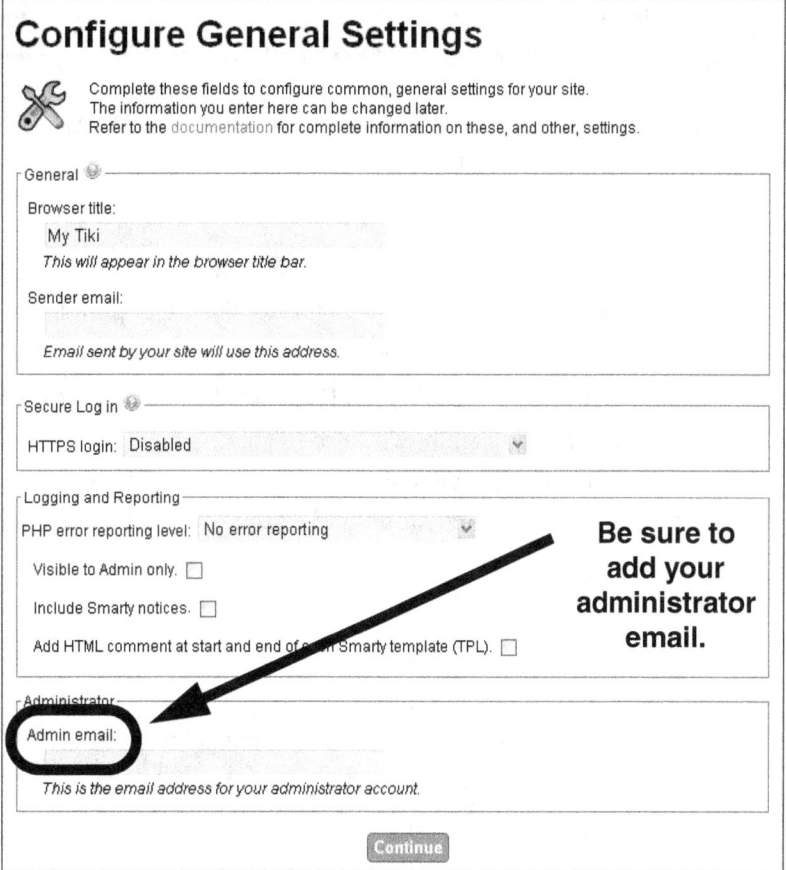

Tip   *Use the **Logging and Reporting** options to assist in troubleshooting, if you encounter errors or problems.*

11. On the **Enter Your Tiki** page, click **Enter Your Tiki and Lock the Installer**.

FIGURE 2.13 *Entering your Tiki*

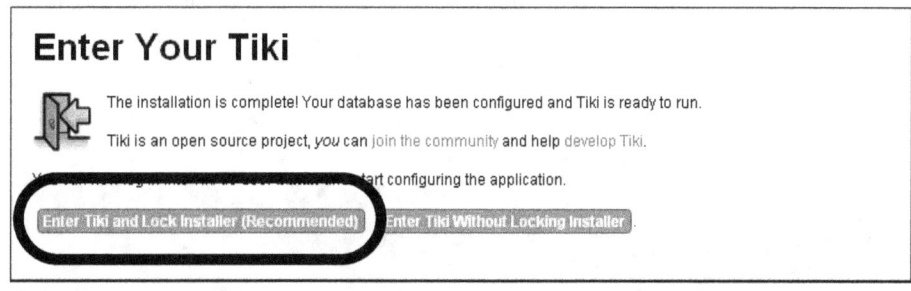

Warning   *Locking the installer helps to protect your Tiki. You can always re-enable the install script, if necessary.*

PERFORMING A MANUAL INSTALLATION

In most instances, the Tiki Installer will successfully install and configure Tiki. However, in some situations you may need to perform a manual installation

Tip *See* *http://doc.tiki.org/Manual+Installation for details on performing a manual installation.*

To install Tiki manually:

1. Create a new MySQL database for Tiki.
2. Create a database user with full administrator permissions to the database.
3. Assign the database user to the newly created database.
4. Download Tiki by using the **Download** link on **http://tiki.org**.
5. Upload (or unzip) the Tiki files to your host.
6. Execute the **../db/tiki.sql** SQL script on your database.
7. Edit (or create) the **../db/local.php** file to include the following:

Tiki local.php file

```
<?php
$db_tiki='mysqli';
$dbversion_tiki='6.0';
$host_tiki='localhost';
$user_tiki='NAME OF YOUR DATABASE USER';
$pass_tiki='PASSWORD FOR YOUR DATABASE USER';
$dbs_tiki='NAME OF YOUR DATABASE';
$client_charset='utf8';
```

Note *If the database is on a different machine from the Web server, replace **localhost** with the URL location of the database.*

By default, Tiki uses UTF-8 for your database encoding. If you select a different encoding method, you must change the **$client_charset** setting to match your database. See "Creating the database" on page 8 for more information.

You should now be able to access your site and log in.

Upgrading your Tiki

Upgrading an existing Tiki site is similar to installing a new site. In fact, you'll use the same Tiki Installer (**tiki-install.php**) that you used to *install* Tiki.

Warning *Always back up your Tiki files and database before upgrading. See "Backing up your Tiki" on page 22 for details.*

Upgrading is essentially a three-step process:

1. Back up your existing site information.
2. Unpack (or copy) the Tiki archive/files to your web server.
3. Run the Tiki Installer, selecting the **Upgrade** option.

There are two ways to upgrade your Tiki: by

- upgrading to the current release

or

- getting the latest code from the repository

Upgrading to the current release

New Tiki releases are announced on **http://tiki.org**. To keep your Tiki safe, always upgrade to the current, stable release.

In this section you will learn about:

- using a patchset
- installing the full version
- restoring your customizations

USING A PATCHSET

For incremental Tiki releases (such as from Version 5.2 to 5.3), you can download a patchset that contains only the files and database definitions that have been changed.

Warning *Be sure to back up your customizations before installing a patchset.*

FIGURE 2.14 *The **5.2to5.3** patchset contains* only *the changes required to move from Tiki 5.2 to 5.3.*

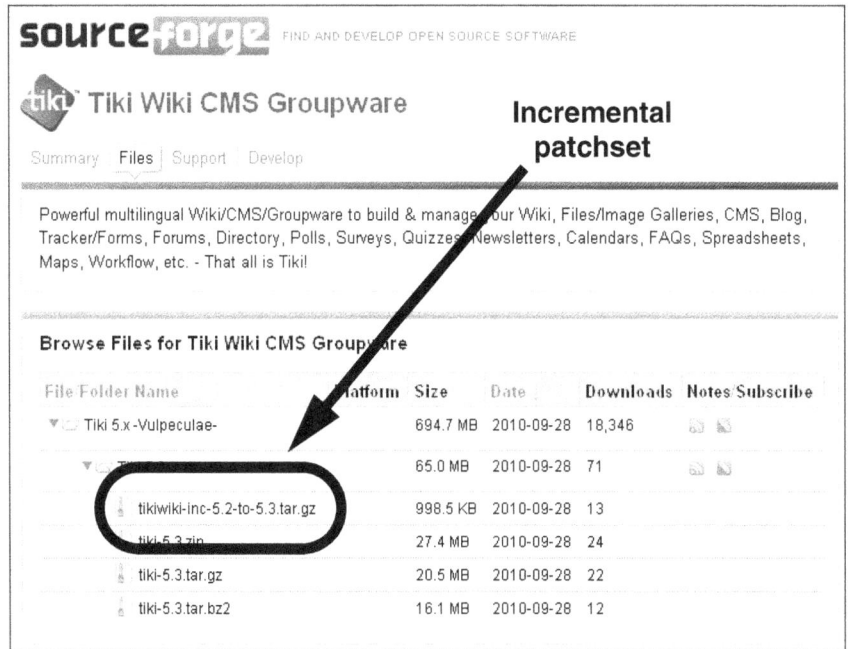

To install the patchset:

1. Download the patchset from SourceForge.net.
2. Unpack the archive into your Tiki directory. The new files will automatically overwrite the existing files.
3. Locate the version-specific **.sql** file in the **.../db** folder and execute it against your database.

Tip *Not all patchsets will contain database changes.*

4. Use the Tiki Installer and select the **Upgrade** option as shown in Figure 2.15 on page 19.

INSTALLING THE FULL VERSION

You can also upgrade your Tiki by installing the latest, full version.

Warning *Be sure to back up your customizations first before running the Tiki Installer. See "Backing up your Tiki" on page 22.*

1. Download the Tiki release, upload (or unzip) the Tiki files to your host, and open your web browser to: **http://*YOUR DOMAIN*/tiki-index.php**. See "Using the Tiki Installer" on page 10 for details.

Tip *You will need your database username and password to complete the **Security Precaution** page and "unlock" the installer.*

2. Tiki should automatically detect that you are upgrading an existing site. Click the link to go directly to the **Install/Upgrade** step.

Note *If the Tiki installer does not display the **Upgrade** link, confirm that the database information in your **../db/local.php** file is correct.*

FIGURE 2.15 *Detecting the upgrade*

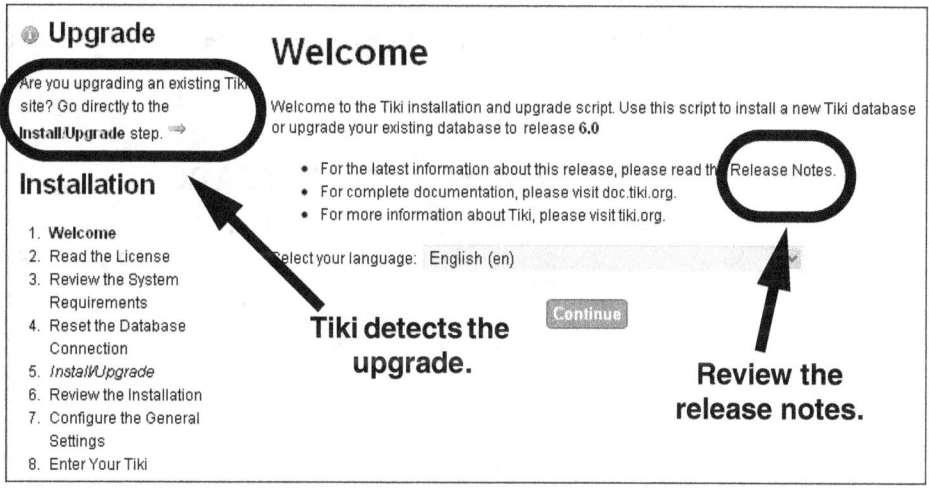

Tip *Review the **release notes** for important upgrade information.*

3. On the **Install & Upgrade** page, click **Upgrade** to upgrade your Tiki database to the current release.

FIGURE 2.16 *Upgrading your database*

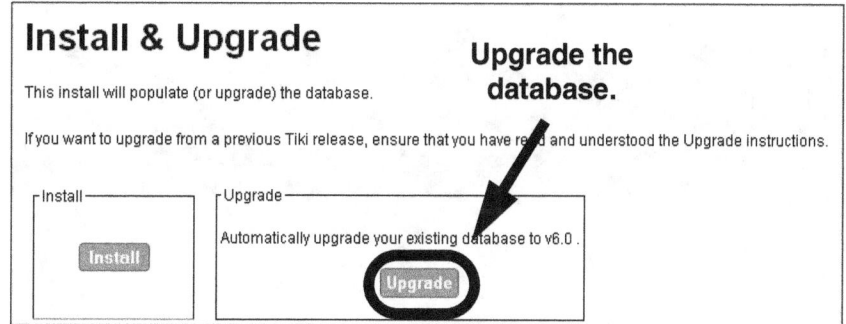

4. On the **Review the Upgrade** page, confirm that all queries were completed successfully and click **Continue**.

FIGURE 2.17 *Completing the upgrade*

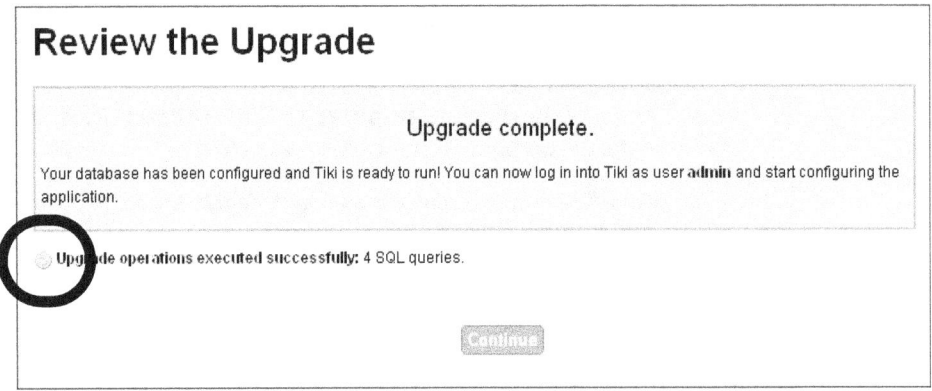

5. Complete the remaining pages of the Tiki Installer, as needed, and enter your Tiki.

   Be sure to read the release notes for each new release, to understand the changes in each.

RESTORING YOUR CUSTOMIZATIONS

After completing your upgrade, you must restore any of the customizations that you previously backed up (see "Backing up your Tiki" on page 22). This includes:

- templates and stylesheets
- file galleries
- attachments
- language files
- plugins and modules

Note *If you customized any PHP files that were part of the upgrade, you must manually copy your customizations to the new version files.*

To avoid this issue, consider joining the Tiki Community (see "Joining the Tiki Community" on page 109) and contributing your customizations to the Tiki code repository.

Getting the latest code from the repository

Did you know that the Tiki Community averages code changes *every two hours*? With development racing along at that speed, it can be tough to stay up to date. In this section, you'll learn how to:

- checkout the latest code from the Subversion (SVN) repository
- become a developer and contribute your own code
- download a daily, pre-built archives

Warning *These daily archives include pre-released code. You should not use the code for a live, in-production site.*

CHECKING OUT FROM SVN

You can check out Tiki code with anonymous access. For example, to check out the latest stable branch, use the following command:

```
svn co https://tikiwiki.svn.sourceforge.net/svnroot/tikiwiki/branches/X.X
```

Where X.X is the version number to check out (such as **6.x**)

To use the current development branch, use:

```
svn co https://tikiwiki.svn.sourceforge.net/svnroot/tikiwiki/trunk
```

If you prefer a GUI SVN client, you can use an application such as Tortoise SVN (**http://tortoisesvn.net**) to check out Tiki code from SVN.

Note *See ⟨⟩ http://dev.tiki.org/SVNTips for additional information on using SVN.*

Become a developer

To check files *into* the repository, you'll need to join the Tiki Community and get committer access. It's quick and easy, and allows you to directly affect the growth of Tiki Wiki CMS Groupware.

See "Joining the Tiki Community" on page 109 for details.

USING PRE-BUILT ARCHIVES

Every six hours, Tiki automatically creates an installable archive (in TAR and ZIP formats) from the latest code. As an alternative to using SVN, you can download these archives, to test or try out the latest, pre-release code.

You can obtain daily builds from: ⟨⟩ **http://dev.tiki.org/Daily+Build**.

Backing up your Tiki

Performing regular backups should be part of ongoing maintenance for your Tiki. In addition to recovering from a disaster, backups are also essential if you move your Tiki to a different host.

Tip *You should perform regular backups of both your database and the files in the Tiki directory. Be sure to test and confirm your backups by restoring them.*

This section includes information on how to back up your Tiki, including:

- saving your theme
- backing up other customizations

SAVING YOUR THEME

If you have customized the *theme* (that is, the skin) of your Tiki, you'll want to be sure to back up all the necessary images and style sheets.

- Your stylesheet is located in **.../styles/YOUR_THEME.css**.
- Graphics and additional files are located in **.../styles/YOUR_THEME/...**
- If you customized any Smarty template TPL files, be sure to back them up as well. Your customized templates are located in **.../templates/styles/YOUR_THEME/...**

BACKING UP OTHER CUSTOMIZATIONS

In addition to the database and theme-specific files, there are other files that you should back up:

- wiki images and attachments
- file galleries
- tracker attachments
- language (translation) files
- plugins
- modules

Note *If you use Tiki Image Galleries (which were deprecated in Tiki 4) and store the images in a directory, you must back up the specific directory, too.*
See **http://doc.tiki.org/Image+Gallery** *for details.*

Tip *Tiki can automatically generate a ZIP files of the necessary files and directories from the* **Tiki Cache/System Admin** *page.*

FIGURE 2.18 *Directories to back up*

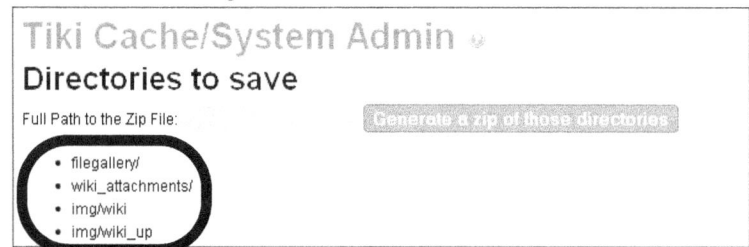

Wiki images

When configuring the Tiki wiki features, you can specify if Tiki uses the File Gallery to store uploaded images.

- If you *do not* use File Galleries to store wiki images and pictures, Tiki stores your uploaded wiki images in the **.../img/wiki_up/...** directory. Be sure to backup this directory.

- If you *do* use File Galleries to store wiki images and pictures, see page 2-24.

FIGURE 2.19 *Configuring the Wiki image location*

Wiki attachments

When configuring the Tiki wiki features, if you use **Attachments** you can specify whether Tiki stores the attachments in the **Database** or in a **Directory**. If you store files in a directory, you must backup the specific directory.

Tip   *Files stored in the* database *are automatically saved when you back up the database.*

FIGURE 2.20   *Configuring the Wiki attachment locations*

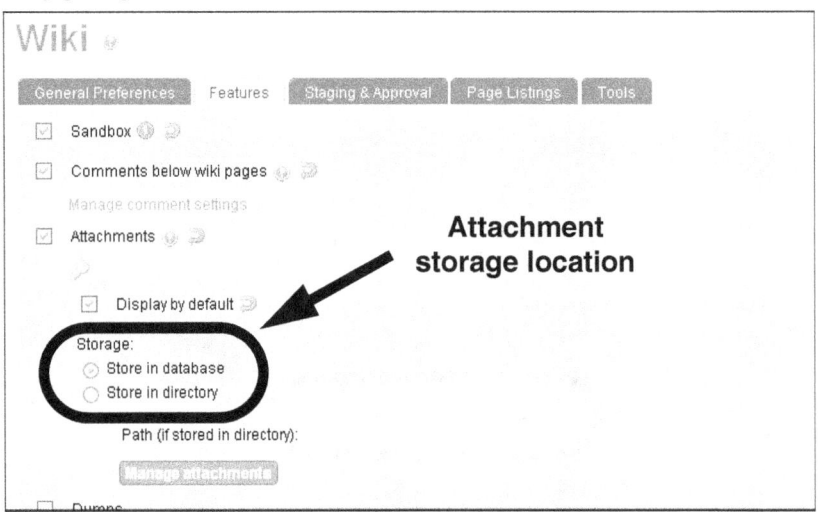

File galleries

When configuring the Tiki File Gallery, you can specify whether Tiki stores files in the **Database** or in a **Directory**. If you store files in a directory, you must back up the specific directory.

Tip   *Files stored in the database are automatically included when you back up the database.*

FIGURE 2.21   *Configuring File Gallery storage location*

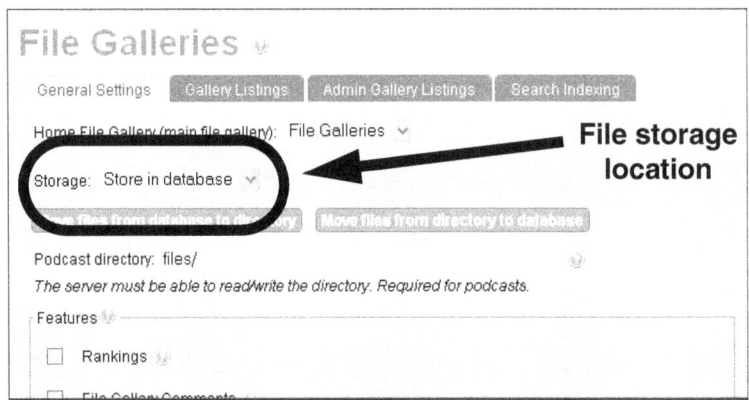

Tracker attachments

When configuring Tiki trackers, you can specify whether Tiki stores the attachments in the **Database** or in a **Directory**. If you store files in a directory, you must backup the specific directory.

Tip *Files stored in the database are automatically included when you back up the database.*

FIGURE 2.22 *Configuring Tracker attachment locations*

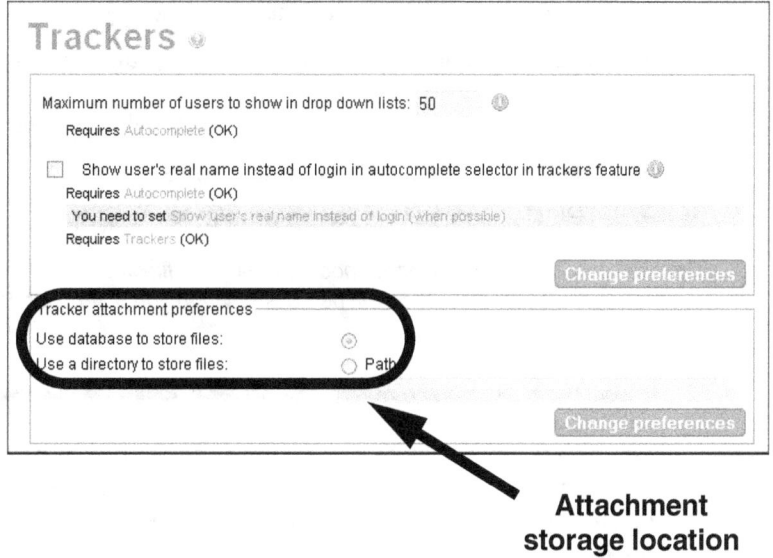

Attachment storage location

Language (Translation) files

You can specify whether Tiki uses the database for interactive translation. If you *do not* use the database, you must backup the specific language files. The files that control the main interface language for Tiki are located in **.../lang/LANGUAGE_ABBREVIATION/*.php**. Instead of customizing the main language file, you can create a **custom.php** file for each language that contains any customized, translated strings. If you created this **custom.php** file you'll need to back it up, too.

Note *See* **http://docs.tiki.org/i18n** *for details on customizing the Tiki language files.*

Tip *You do not need to perform any special handling to backup the translations of specific wiki pages or articles. These will be included in the database backup.*

Plugins and modules

If you created any custom wiki plugins or modules (or modified exiting items), you will need to back up those files, too. If you have made updates, fixes, or enhancements to Tiki plugins and modules, please consider sharing your work back with the Tiki Community. It is easy to contribute your work. See "Joining the Tiki Community" on page 109 for details.

Normally, there are two files for each *plugin* that you will need to back up:

- a PHP file, located in **.../lib/wiki-plugins/*.php**
- a TPL file, located in **.../templates/wiki-plugins/*.tpl**

Normally, there are two files for each *module* that you will need to back up:

- a PHP file, located in **.../modules/*.php**
- a TPL file, located in **.../templates/modules/*.tpl**

Tip   *You can include customized module templates files as part of your own template customizations. If so, they will be backed when you save your theme.*

Anything else

Normally, you should not need to edit or modify any PHP files. If you have customized any of the Tiki application libraries or files, you'll need to back them up as well.

If you made improvements or fixed issues with your changes, please consider contributing your changes to the Tiki source code. It is quick and easy, and helps you to avoid having a "forked" version that will be difficult to maintain and upgrade. This is also good for the Tiki community, since it accelerates Tiki's progress and overall development. See "Joining the Tiki Community" on page 109.

BACKING UP THE DATABASE

The MySQL database used by Tiki contains all of the "data" for your site, including:

- all Tiki feature items (such as wiki pages, articles, polls, and so on)
- menus and menu options
- site preferences and settings

Using phpMyAdmin

If you use phpMyAdmin, the easiest way to back up your database is to use the **Export** feature in phpMyAdmin.

FIGURE 2.23 *Exporting the database*

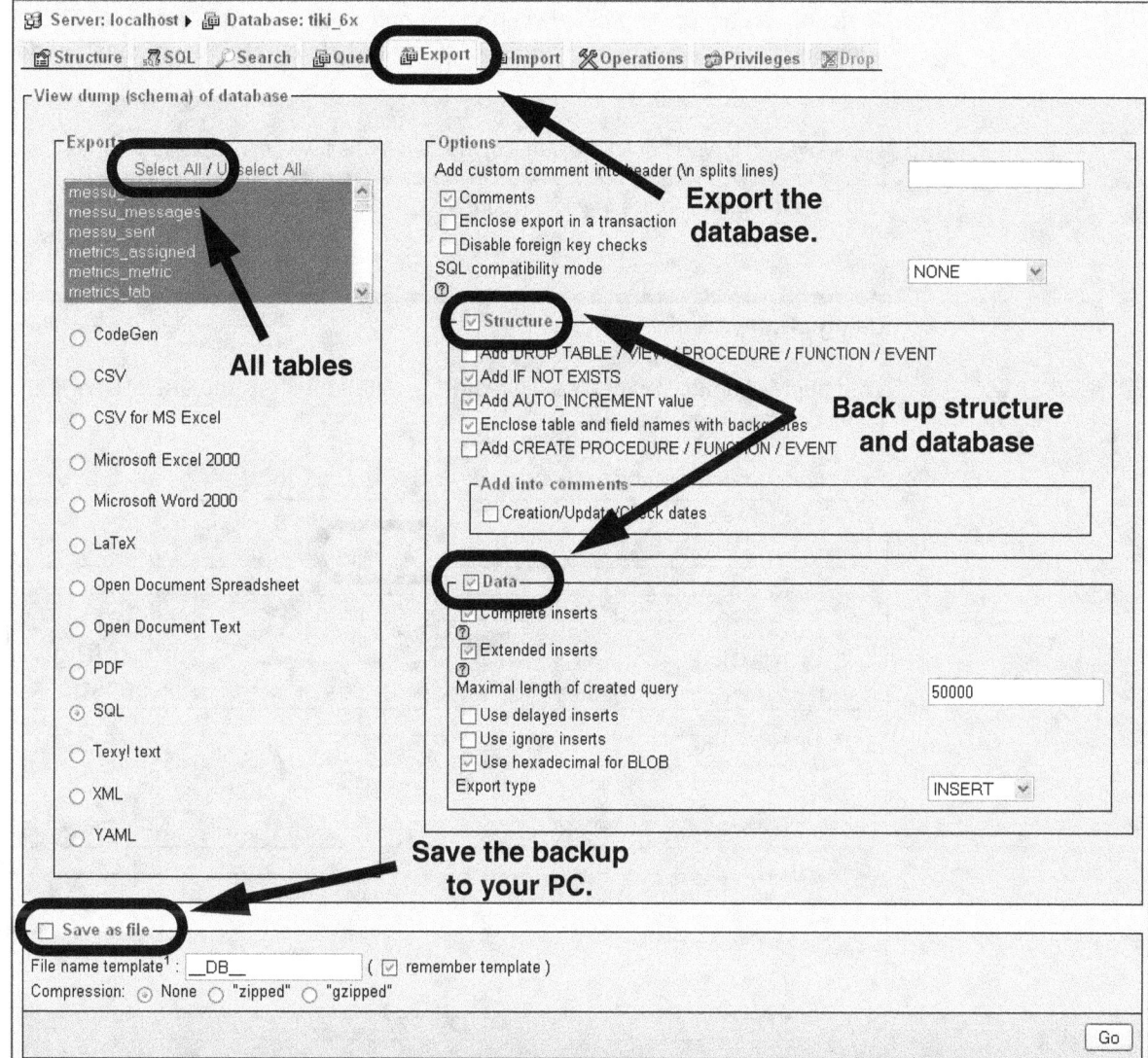

The resulting **.sql** file (or archived format, if you selected **zip** or **gzip** format) contains the complete database. With it, you can restore the database — and your entire Tiki.

Tip *For detailed information on using phpMyAdmin, see **http://www.phpmyadmin.net**.*

Using the command line

You can also back up your database from a command line by using the following command to create a "dump" of the database:

```
mysqldump DATABSE_NAME > DUMP_FILE
```

Tip *For detailed information on using mySQL, see **http://www.mysql.com**.*

RESTORING FROM A BACKUP

To restore a backup, you simply import the dump file into your database. The dump file contains the necessary SQL commands to create the database and populate it.

Tip *Depending on the size of your database, the SQL transaction may exceed your host's maximum allowed value. You may need to increase the **max_execution_time** and **max_input_time** variables in your **php.ini** file.*

Using phpMyAdmin

With phpMyAdmin, you can easily restore a database by using the **Import** feature to import the dump file.

FIGURE 2.24   *Importing a previously created backup file.*

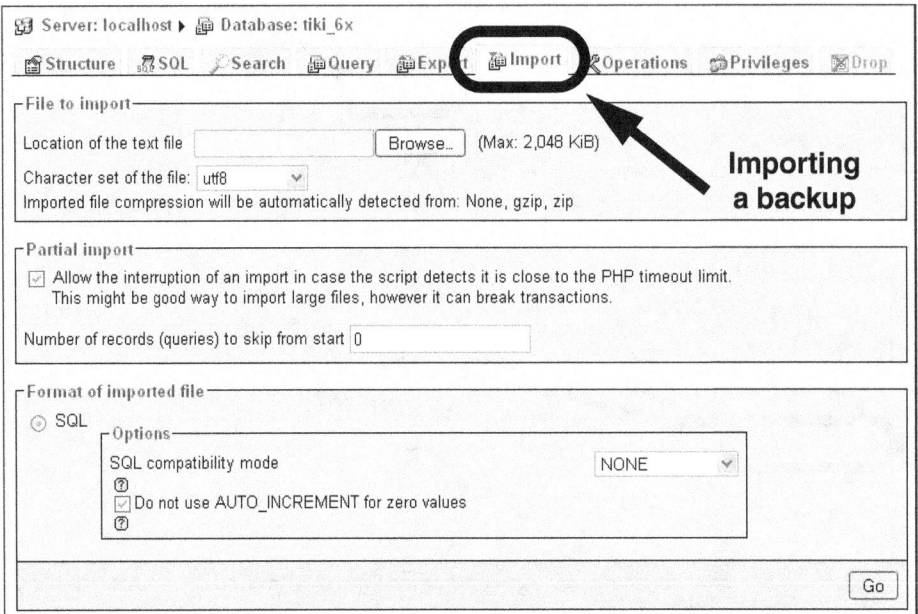

Simply select the backup dump file that you create previously. See "Backing up the database" on page 26.

Using the command line

To restore a database from a dump file from the command line, use the following command:

```
mysql.exe -u DATABASE_USERNAME -p DATABASE_NAME < DUMP_FILE
```

CHAPTER 3

Customizing Tiki Themes, Styles, and Templates

Because Tiki separates the application logic (the PHP files) from the presentation layer (the Smarty TPL files), it is very easy to customize the look and feel of your Tiki site. Tiki includes several themes (or skins) to choose from, but you can easily create your own.

FIGURE 3.25 *Tiki Themes is your headquarters for fabulous looking themes.*

The Tiki Themes site has an extensive list of template tricks that can help you customize your theme. See 🌐 **http://themes.tiki.org/Template+Tricks** for details.

IN THIS CHAPTER

Using the Look and Feel

The **General** tab of the **Admin: Look & Feel** page is very powerful. By using the options on this tab, you can customize nearly every aspect of your site's theme—all from within Tiki. There's no need to edit files or transfer items to your host!

This is especially helpful in "future proofing" your site. Since your changes are maintained within the database, you will not have to duplicate your custom edits each time you upgrade.

This section includes information on adding custom CSS (Cascading Style Sheets) styles to your site.

Tip *For complete information on using CSS, see **http://www.w3.org/Style/CSS**.*

ADDING CUSTOM CSS STYLES

There are two ways to add custom CSS styles to your Tiki:

- including an additional CSS
- using inline styles

Later, you'll see how to add these styles on a per-page basis.

Including an additional CSS

If you already have custom styles in a CSS style sheet, you can easily add the CSS file to Tiki.

1. Copy your **.css** file to your Web server. You could FTP the file, or even use Tiki's file gallery to store the file.

Note *Storing CSS files in the Tiki file gallery may cause performance issues.*

2. On the **General Layout Options** tab of the **Admin: Look & Feel** page, add the following to the **Custom HTML <head> Content** area:

Including a CSS file

```
<link rel="stylesheet" href="DIRECTORY/FILENAME.css" type="text/css" media="screen" />
```

FIGURE 3.26 *Adding a CSS file*

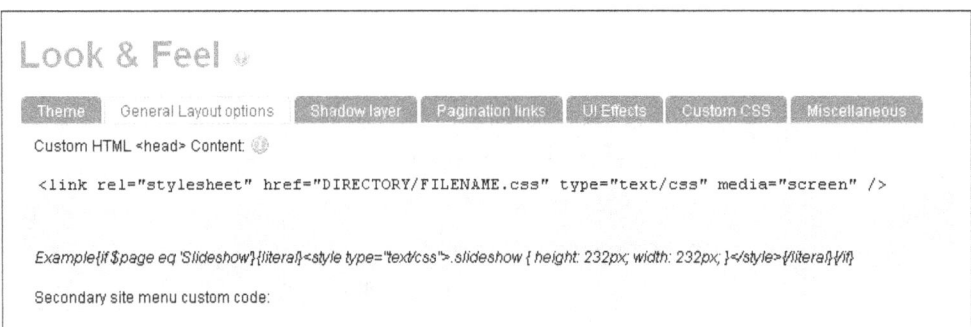

3. Click **Apply**.

4. Clear the Tiki caches.

You can now use any of the styles from your custom **.css** file in a Tiki wiki page. For example, you could use the **DIV** plugin:

Using a custom CSS style

```
{DIV(class="CUSTOM_CSS_CLASS")}
   This text will be styled with the CUSTOM_CSS_CLASS.
{DIV}
```

Using inline styles

If you do not have a completed CSS file, you can create custom CSS styles in Tiki.

1. On the **Admin: Look & Feel** page, click the **Custom CSS** tab.

2. In the **Custom Code** area, add your CSS definitions in the **Custom CSS** area.

Including a CSS file

```
.CUSTOM_CSS_CLASS {
      padding:1em, font-size:2.0em; font-weight:bold
}
```

FIGURE 3.27 *Custom CSS style definitions*

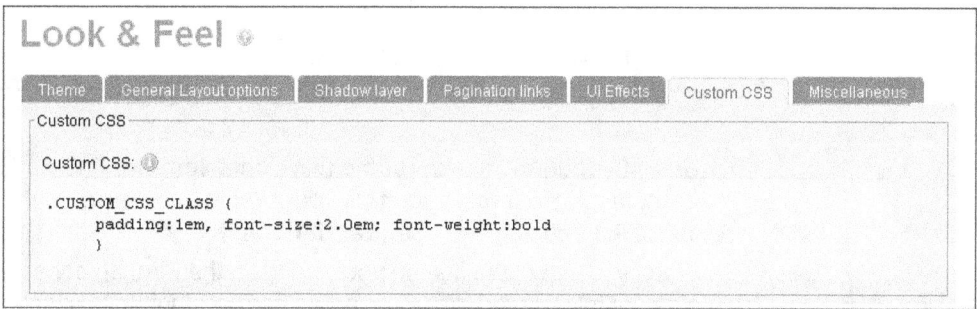

3. Click **Apply**.

4. Clear all Tiki caches.

You can now use any of the styles in your custom **.css** file in Tiki. For example, you could use the **DIV** plugin:

Using a custom CSS style

```
{DIV(class="CUSTOM_CSS_CLASS")}
   This text will be styled with the CUSTOM_CSS_CLASS.
{DIV}
```

Now that you know *how* to customize specific CSS styles, how can you determine *which* CSS style to edit?

Determining which CSS style to edit

If you review the HTML source of a Tiki site, you'll see that it uses hundreds of CSS styles for everything from the title of a blog post to a wiki page description to a module title. Additionally, an average Tiki site may use styles from multiple CSS files.

When customizing your Tiki theme, how can you determine which styles to change? By using a Web browser utility such as Firebug (for Firefox) or the IE Developer Tools (for Internet Explorer).

For example, assume that you want to customize the size, color, and font of the default Tiki **<h2>** heading:

FIGURE 3.28   *The default <h2> heading*

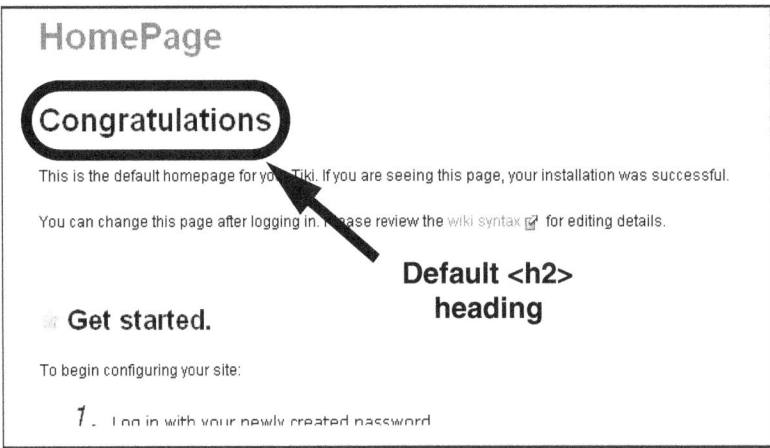

1. Using Firebug for Firefox (or the Developer Tools for Internet Explorer), select an element on a Tiki wiki page that you want to customize. In this example, we'll select the heading text **Congratulations**.
2. When you select the item in your browser, the Firebug console displays the HTML element information for the selected item, including its styles, as shown in Figure 3.29 on page 33.

   Notice that the **Congratulations** text is defined by the **h2** element. Notice, too, that the element gets some attributes from the **fivealive.css** style sheet and others from the **lite.css** style sheet.

FIGURE 3.29 *The selected item's element and attributes*

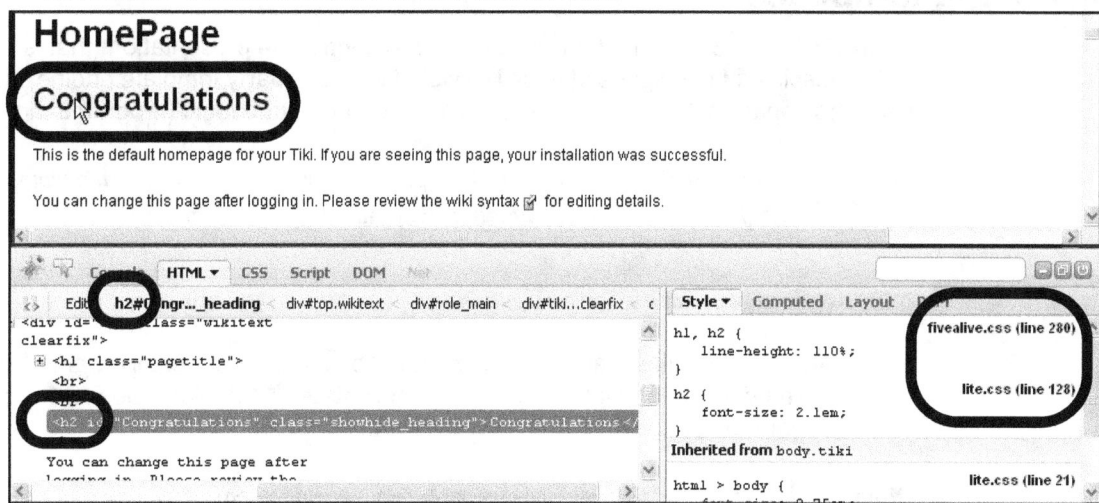

3. Using one of the methods described in "Adding custom CSS styles" on page 30, create a new definition for the **h2** element:

Customizing the H2 element

```
h2 {
    font-size:3.0em;
    color:#ffff00;
    font-family: serif;
    }
```

4. Reload the home page of your Tiki. The **<h2>** headings are now larger, yellow, and in a serif font.

FIGURE 3.30 *Your new, customized heading*

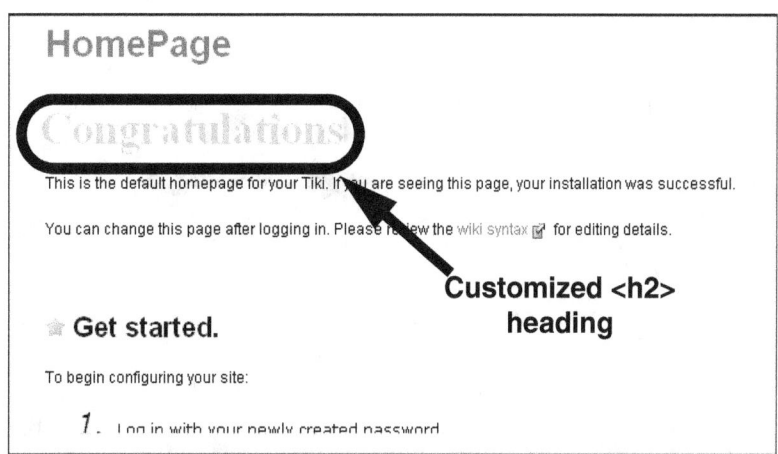

Note *You may need to clear the Tiki cache and your browser's cache to see the new style.*

Modifying templates

Tiki uses Smarty (TPL) template files to control the presentation (that is, the display) of each page of your Tiki website. The Smarty template engine allows you to separate the presentation (look and feel) from the logic (programming).

Note *Do not confuse these Smarty (TPL) template files with the Tiki content templates. See* 🔅 *http://doc.tiki.org/Content+Template for more information.*

Tip *For complete information on using Smarty, see **http://www.smarty.net**.*

Any template files that you modify should be placed in a custom theme folder—do not modify the template files in the **.../templates/*.tpl** folder. See "Saving your Theme" on page 22 for more information.

Note *Creating modified template files as part of your custom theme may make it more difficult to upgrade your Tiki. You will need to re-apply your customizations to the new set of templates each time you upgrade.*

FINDING THE RIGHT TEMPLATE

So, how do you figure out which of the more than 800 template (TPL) files you need to edit? Some template files have a direct, one-to-one correlation with a PHP file. This means you simply need to look at the browser's address bar to determine the correct template.

For example, the template used for the site registration page (**tiki-register.php**) is **tiki-register.tpl**.

FIGURE 3.31 *One template per page*

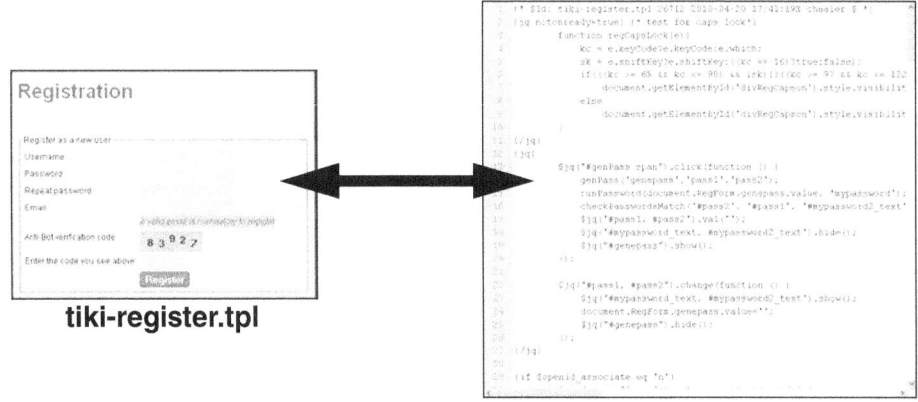

tiki-register.tpl

tiki-register.php

For other pages it is not nearly that easy. Some pages, such as the event calendar (**tiki-calendar.php**), are actually made up of five (or more!) templates. Luckily, there is an option to help you find which templates are used.

When you enable the **Smarty Template usage indicator** option on the **Theme** tab of the **Admin: Look & Feel** page, Tiki will add comments to the generated HTML files to identify the beginning and ending of each template (TPL) file.

FIGURE 3.32   *Enabling the template indicator*

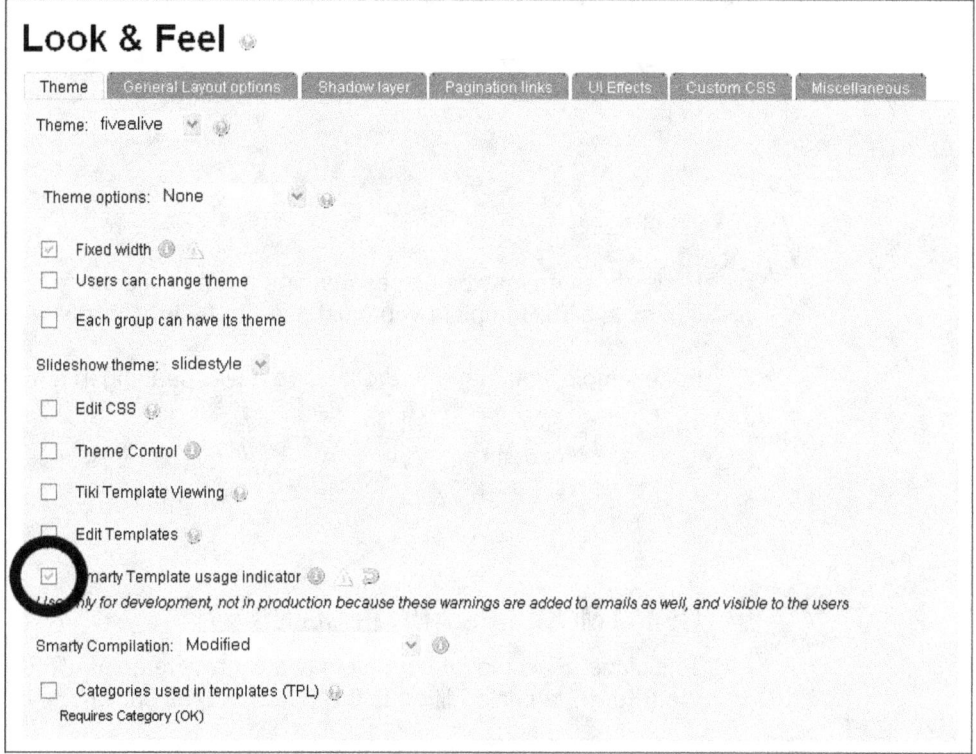

By viewing the HTML source of a generated Tiki page, you can determine which template (TPL) is responsible for what content, as shown below:

FIGURE 3.33   *Template comments*

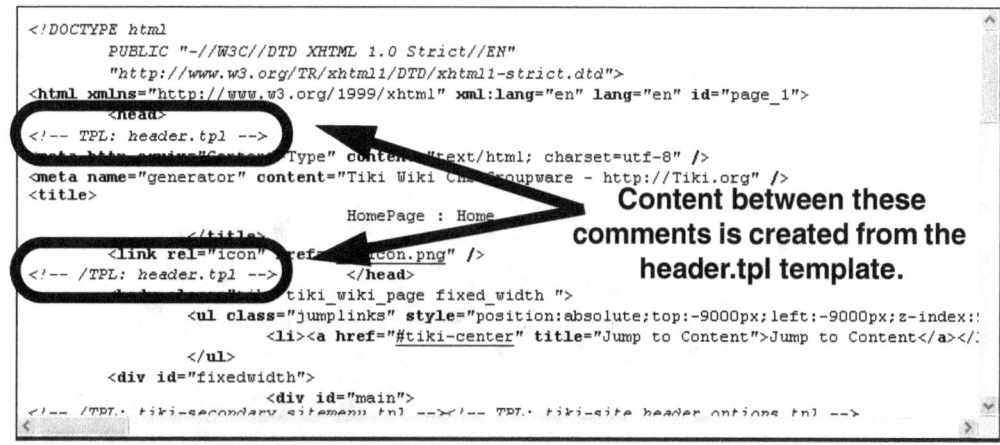

Warning   *Do not use the **Smarty Template usage indicator** on a "live" site. Tiki will include the template comments in all generated content, including messages and email, and these comments will be visible to all site users.*

INCLUDING WIKI SYNTAX

The Tiki template (TPL) files are created with the Smarty template engine. Smarty templates use a mixture of XHTML and PHP—not Tiki's wiki syntax.

Note *See* **http://doc.tiki.org/Wiki+Syntax** *for details about wiki syntax.*

For example, to bold text in a Smarty TPL template file, use:

```
<strong>text</strong>
```

not:

```
__text__
```

However, there may be places that you need to use some wiki syntax. To use wiki syntax in a Tiki template you must use the **{wiki}** Smarty tag.

For example, you may want to include a wiki heading in template. Use:

```
{wiki}
!Level 1 Heading
...
{/wiki}
```

USING MODULES AND PLUGINS

To include a Tiki module or plugin in a Smarty template (TPL) file, you must use the **{literal}** tag, in addition to the **{wiki}** tag, as shown previously.

For example, if you wanted to include the Tiki search module at the bottom of every Web page on your Tiki site, you could add the following to the **footer.tpl** template:

Adding the Search module to a template

```
{wiki}
  {literal}
    {MODULE(module=>search, show_object_filter=y,
advanced_search=y) /}
  {/literal}
{/wiki}
```

Tip *You could also use the simplified version of the module:*
```
{module module=search show_object_filter=y advanced_search=y}
```

When adding plugins, you can use the **{wikiplugin}** tag to avoid having to use the **{wiki}** and **{literal}** tags:

Adding a wiki plugin to a template

```
{wikiplugin _name="NAME OF PLUGIN" PARAMETER="VALUE"
PARAMETER="VALUE"}{/wikiplugin}
```

See "Using modules" on page 50 for additional information about Tiki modules.

Making other customizations

In addition to customizing the site look and feel of your Tiki by modifying its templates or using the **Admin: Look & Feel** options, you can make custom changes on a per-page or per-category basis.

In this section, you will learn:

- customizing per page
- customizing by category

Tip *You can also use modules on a per-page or per-category basis. See "Using modules" on page 50 for more information.*

CUSTOMIZING PER PAGE

Previously, you saw how to add new CSS styles to Tiki. While this method works well, it can add additional "overhead" to your site: Why load all those custom styles, if you only need to use them on specific pages?

If you included a custom CSS file in the **Custom HTML Content** area on the **General Layout Options** tab of the **Admin: Look & Feel** page, you can tell Tiki to only load the file for a specific page:

FIGURE 3.34 *Adding a conditional CSS file*

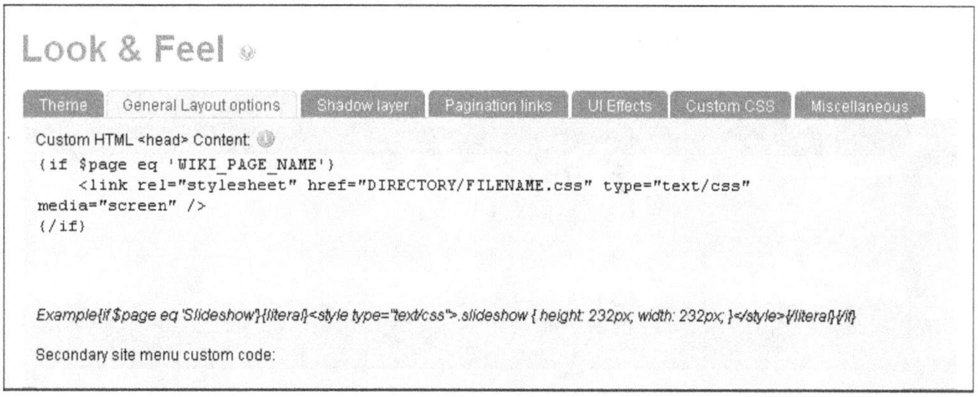

```
Look & Feel

Theme   General Layout options   Shadow layer   Pagination links   UI Effects   Custom CSS   Miscellaneous

Custom HTML <head> Content:
{if $page eq 'WIKI_PAGE_NAME'}
    <link rel="stylesheet" href="DIRECTORY/FILENAME.css" type="text/css"
media="screen" />
{/if}


Example{if $page eq 'Slideshow'}{literal}<style type="text/css">.slideshow { height: 232px; width: 232px; }</style>{/literal}{/if}

Secondary site menu custom code:
```

Including a CSS file

```
{if $page eq 'WIKI_PAGE_NAME'}
    <link rel="stylesheet" href="DIRECTORY/FILENAME.css"
type="text/css" media="screen" />
{/if}
```

Note *The {if} notation is an example of using Smarty and PHP syntax. See "Modifying templates" on page 34 for more information.*

Likewise, if you use the **Custom CSS** tab to include inline styles, you can also make those styles conditional:

Including CSS styles

```
{if $page eq 'WIKI_PAGE_NAME'}
    .CUSTOM_CSS_CLASS {
        padding:1em, font-size:2.0em; font-weight:bold
    }
{/if}
```

Note The *$page* variable works only with wiki pages.

CUSTOMIZING BY CATEGORY

In addition to customizing per page, you can use customized styles for specific categories.

Note See  **http://doc.tiki.org/Category** for details about Tiki categories.

To allow Tiki to use category information and IDs in templates and styles, you must first enable the **Categories used in templates** option on the **Admin: Categories** page:

FIGURE 3.35 *Enabling the use of Category IDs in templates*

Using the same process as before, you can create an **{if}** statement to check for a specific category ID. For example, to check if the current object is in category **2**, you could use:

```
{if in_array(2, $objectCategoryIds)}
    ...
{/if}
```

CHAPTER 4   *Adding Web Content and Widgets to Tiki Pages*

Tiki Wiki CMS Groupware is a wiki-based content management system. This makes it very easy to add content to your Tiki site. There is plenty of great content on the Internet that you might want to make available on your site. This section explains how.

Note   *Always check with the content owner and applicable copyrights before copying or reproducing existing material.*

IN THIS CHAPTER

Editing wiki pages

One way to add content to a page is by simply editing the wiki page. When editing wiki pages, there are a few special features you should be aware of, such as:

- copying and pasting
- inserting special characters
- using entity values
- using the Special Characters button

COPYING AND PASTING

One of the easiest ways to add content to your Tiki pages is simply to copy from the source material (such as a PDF or DOC file) and paste into a Tiki wiki page. Your results will vary, depending on the Tiki editor that you are using.

Using the WYSIWYG editor

When pasting text into the wiki editor, Tiki will attempt to preserve the formatting, if possible. Additionally, any images that appeared in the original source will be included (via reference).

Note See ⟡ *http://doc.tiki.org/wysiwyg* for complete information on the WYSIWYG editor.

FIGURE 4.36 *Copying text into the WYSIWYG editor will preserve most formatting.*

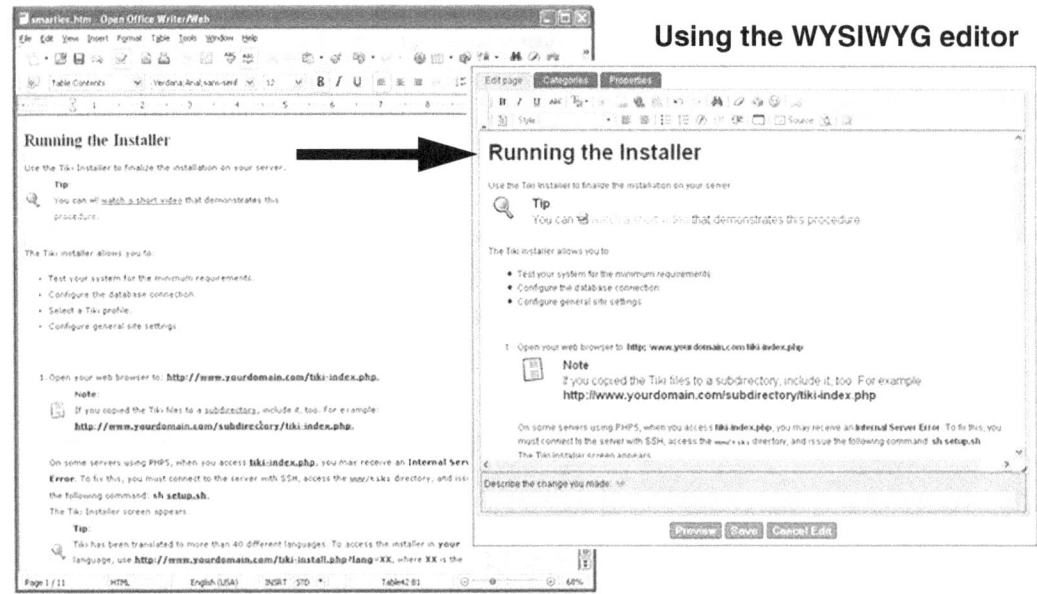

Note *When you paste items into the Tiki WYSIWYG editor, some browsers may display a security message. You can safely disregard it.*

Using the Wiki editor

When pasting text into the wiki editor, Tiki will usually strip out any formatting and special characters. For best results, use the **Paste... as Plain Text** or **Paste... Special** options, if supported by your system's clipboard application.

FIGURE 4.37 *Copying text into the wiki editor will strip all formatting.*

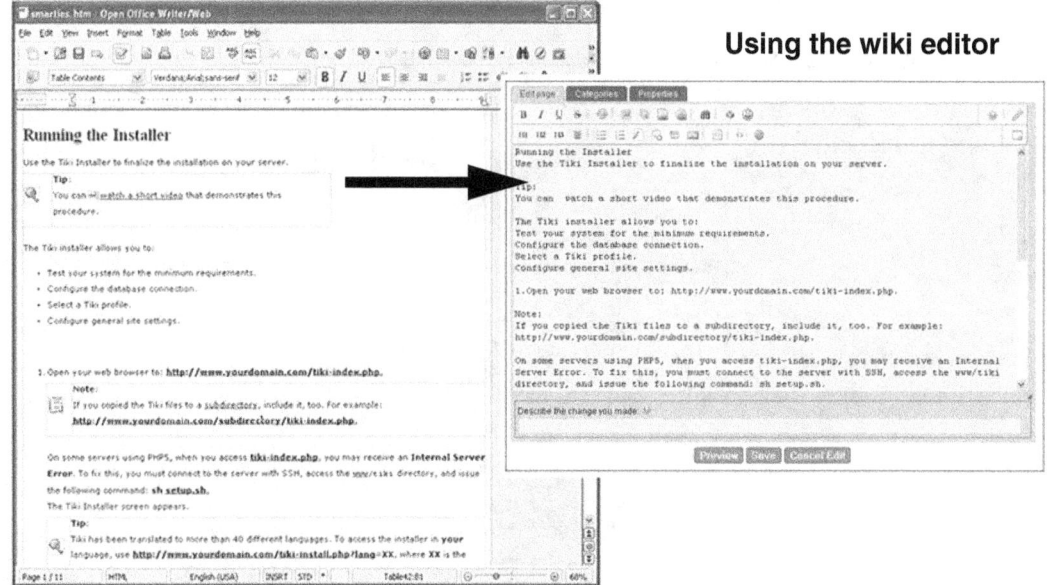

This will preserve line and paragraph breaks, but you will need to re-apply the necessary text formatting and import any images.

INSERTING SPECIAL CHARACTERS

Sometimes, you may want to add a character or symbol that does not exist on your keyboard, such as © or ½. Tiki provides a few methods to add these special characters:

Tip   *To learn about other special characters, see* **http:// doc.tiki.org/Wiki+Syntax**.

Using entity values

The ISO 8859-1 specification is a commonly used character encoding scheme for characters and symbols from the Latin alphabet. You can include any character in a wiki page by using its entity value.

For example, the entity value for the copyright symbol (©) is **169**. To include this symbol in a Tiki wiki page, use: ~**169**~ .

Note   *For full details on HTML entities, see*
http://www.w3.org/TR/REC-html40/sgml/entities.html.

Using the Special Characters button

To insert a special character while editing a page:

1. Click the **Special Character** button. The **Select Special Character** window appears.

Note *This button is available in both the WYSIWYG and Wiki editors.*

FIGURE 4.38   *Selecting special characters (WYSIWYG)*

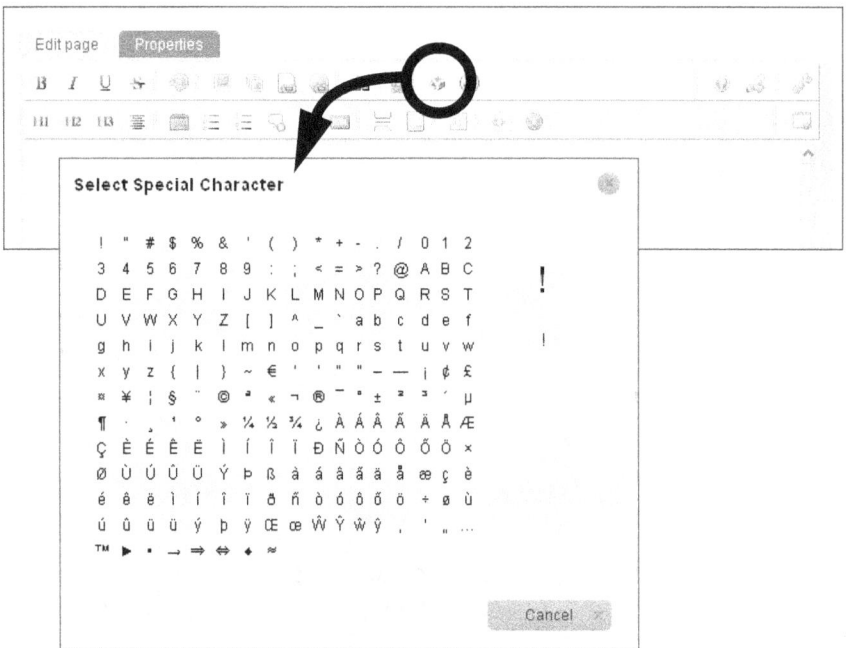

2. Click the character to insert. Tiki inserts the character.

Adding widgets and scripts

Tiki "sanitizes" all text that is added to a wiki page to ensure that no one adds any malicious code or scripts that could attack your site or its visitors.

However, there are many useful scripts that you may want to embed in a wiki page (such as dynamic content, video players, and other "Web 2.0" applications). Normally, these scripts require cutting and pasting custom HTML code or JavaScript.

This section explains how to add these widgets to your Tiki wiki pages by:

- using the HTML plugin
- using the JS plugin

Tip *You can also create a custom plugin or user module in order to add special content.*

Using the HTML plugin

The **HTML** plugin is one of the easiest ways add *anything* to a wiki page. It is extremely powerful.

Note *For complete details on the **HTML** plugin, see* **http://doc.tiki.org/pluginHTML**. *Tiki also includes a number of feature-specific plugins that can be used as an alternative to the **HTML** plugin. See* **http://doc.tiki.org/wiki+plugin** *for details.*

CREATING THE HTML PLUGIN

For example, in order to embed this YouTube video in a wiki page:

FIGURE 4.39 *Tiki Structures video from YouTube (http://www.youtube.com/watch?v=KBewVCducWw)*

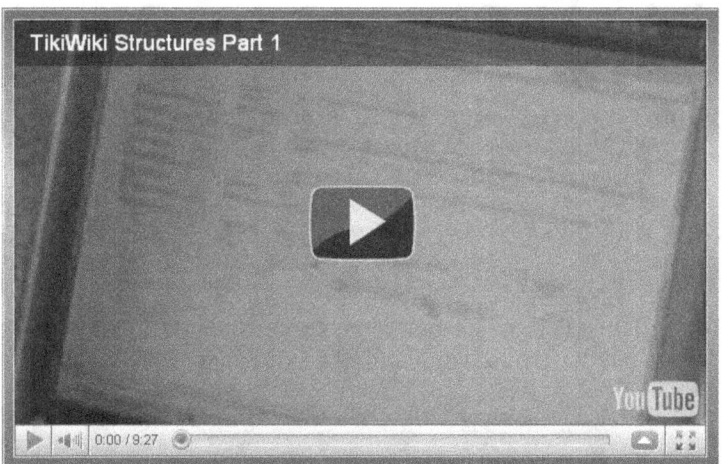

YouTube generates the following code:

YouTube embed script

```
<object width="580" height="360">
  <param name="movie" value="http://www.youtube.com/v/
KBewVCducWw&hl=en_US&fs=1&color1=0x3a3a3a&color2=0x999999&border=1"></param>
  <param name="allowFullScreen" value="true"></param><param name="allowscriptaccess"
value="always"></param>
  <embed src="http://www.youtube.com/v/
KBewVCducWw&hl=en_US&fs=1&color1=0x3a3a3a&color2=0x999999&border=1" type="application/
x-shockwave-flash" allowscriptaccess="always" allowfullscreen="true" width="580"
height="360"></embed>
</object>
```

If you attempt to simply copy and paste this code into a wiki page, Tiki will sanitize the script elements.

Instead, use the **HTML** plugin:

HTML Plugin

```
{HTML()}
<object width="580" height="360">
  <param name="movie" value="http://www.youtube.com/v/
KBewVCducWw&hl=en_US&fs=1&color1=0x3a3a3a&color2=0x999999&border=1"></param>
  <param name="allowFullScreen" value="true"></param><param name="allowscriptaccess"
value="always"></param>
  <embed src="http://www.youtube.com/v/
KBewVCducWw&hl=en_US&fs=1&color1=0x3a3a3a&color2=0x999999&border=1" type="application/
x-shockwave-flash" allowscriptaccess="always" allowfullscreen="true" width="580"
height="360"></embed>
</object>
{HTML}
```

Warning   *The **HTML** plugin will allow you (or anyone with **tiki_p_trust_input** permission) to add any HTML coding to the page; this includes potentially malicious code. Be sure to allow only trusted editors to use this plugin.*

PLUGIN PARAMETERS

The **HTML** plugin contains one optional parameter: **Wiki**. Use this parameter to instruct Tiki to parse any wiki syntax. For example:

HTML Plugin without wiki syntax parsing

```
{HTML()}
This link uses an __onclick__ event to produce a popup window:
 <a href="#" onClick="alert( 'This message is __bold__.' )">
  Click Here
 </a>
{HTML}
```

will produce:

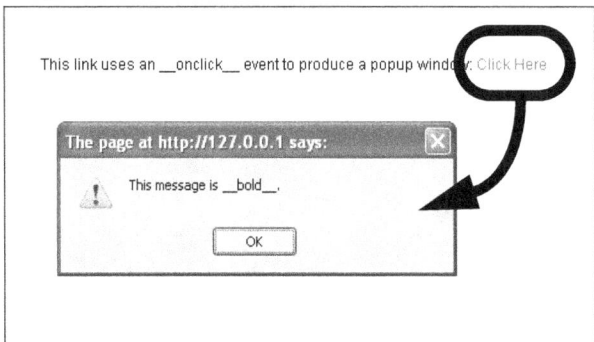

Notice that the text "onclick" and "bold" are ***not*** bold, even though they both include the wiki bold syntax. By default, Tiki will ***not*** parse wiki syntax in the **HTML** plugin.

Use the **Wiki** syntax parameter to tell Tiki to parse the syntax. For example:

HTML Plugin with wiki syntax parsing

```
{HTML(wiki=1)}
This link uses an __onclick__ event to produce a popup window:
 <a href="#" onClick="alert( 'This message is __bold__.' )">
  Click Here
 </a>
{HTML}
```

will produce:

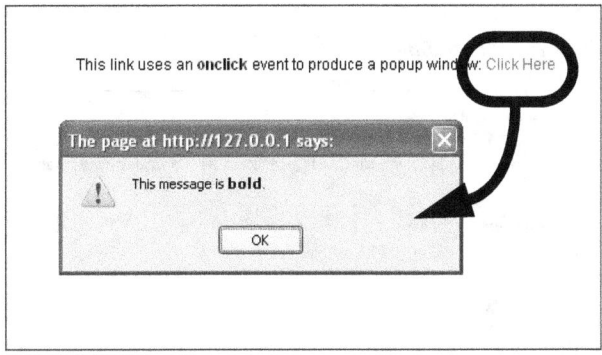

ENABLING THE HTML PLUGIN

Plugins must be enabled before they can be used in wiki page. If you attempt to use a disabled plugin, Tiki displays the following message:

FIGURE 4.40 *Enabling a disabled plugin*

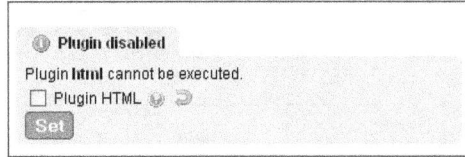

Select the plugin, and click **Set** to enable it.

APPROVING THE HTML PLUGIN

Some plugins require approval before they become "live," especially those, such as the **HTML** plugin, that allow users to embed specific coding. Only users with the necessary permission can approve pending plugins.

Note   *To avoid requiring approval, Tiki provides specialized plugins for specific purposes. See http://doc.tiki.org/Wiki+Plugin for a list of all available plugins.*

To approve a pending **HTML** plugin:

1. Click **View Details.** Tiki displays the details of the **HTML** plugin.

FIGURE 4.41   *Details of the HTML plugin*

2. Select one of the following options:

   - Click **Preview** to execute the plugin once. Tiki reloads the page and executes the plugin. But on subsequent page visits, the plugin will not execute.

   - Click **Approve** to make the plugin "live." Tiki reloads the page, fully executing the plugin code.

   - Click **Reject** to disapprove the plugin and deny its execution. Tiki displays the following message:

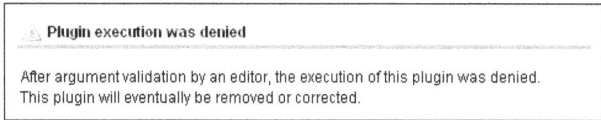

You should edit the page and remove the denied plugin code.

DISPLAYING ALL PENDING PLUGINS

Use the **Plugin Approval** page to display all plugins that are pending approval.

1. On the **Admin: Text Area** page, click the **Plugins** tab.

FIGURE 4.42 *Plugins tab of Admin: Text Area page*

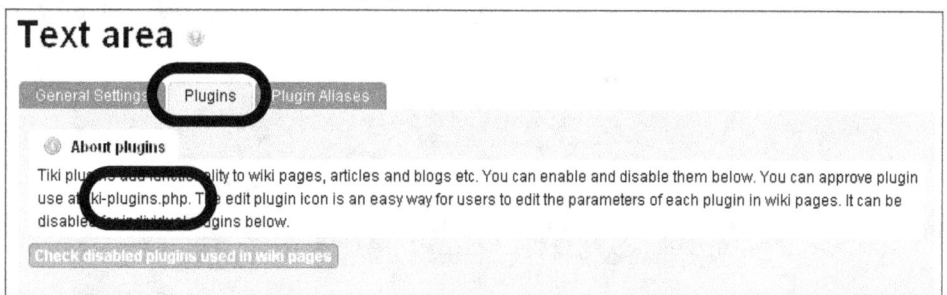

2. Click the **tiki-plugins.php** link.

FIGURE 4.43 *Approving plugins*

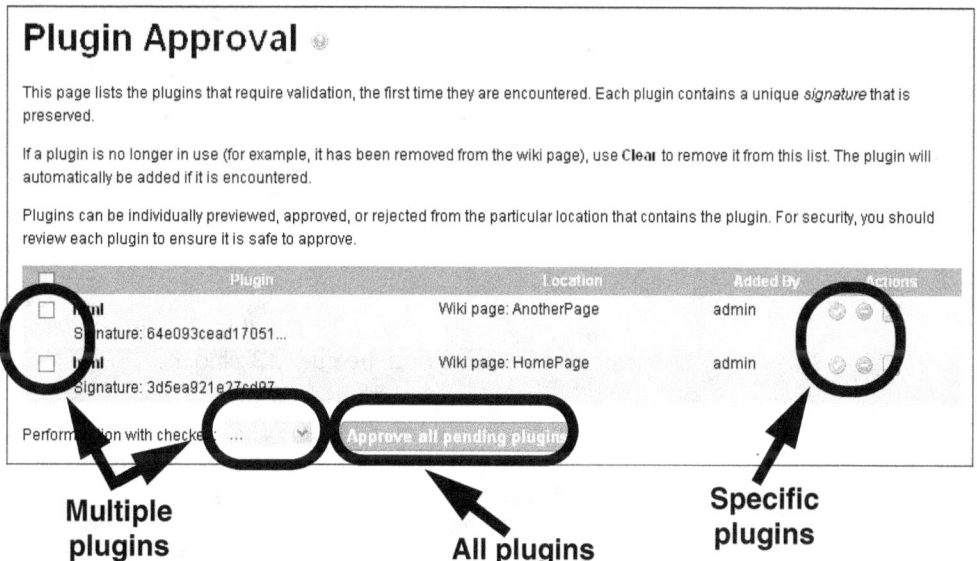

For each pending plugin, Tiki will display:

- the plugin and its unique, security ID
- the location of the page (for plugins included on wiki pages)
- the user who added the plugin or last visited the page

You can approve or deny specific plugins:

- To approve a specific plugin, click **Approve** .
- To reject a specific plugin, click **Clear** .
- To approve or reject specific plugins, select the plugins and select the appropriate action from the droplist.
- To approve *all* pending plugins, click **Approve all pending plugins**.

Using the JS plugin

The **JS** (Javascript) plugin is another very useful one for extending your Tiki. With it, you can easily include <SCRIPT> elements in a wiki page. For example, to embed this widget (from Widgetbox) in a wiki page:

FIGURE 4.44 *RSS widget from Widgetbox (http://www.widgetbox.com/widget/rss)*

Widgetbox generates the following code:

Widgetbox script

```
<script type="text/javascript" src="http://cdn.widgetserver.com/
syndication/subscriber/InsertWidget.js"></script>
<script type="text/javascript">
  if (WIDGETBOX)
    WIDGETBOX.renderWidget('5916c179-aace-43f5-b07a-3ac0df9d8546');
</script>
```

If you attempt to simply copy and paste this code into a wiki page, Tiki will sanitize the script elements. Instead, use the **JS** plugin:

Using JS plugin

```
{JS(file="http://cdn.widgetserver.com/syndication/subscriber/
InsertWidget.js") /}
{JS()}if (WIDGETBOX)
    WIDGETBOX.renderWidget('5916c179-aace-43f5-b07a-3ac0df9d8546');
{JS}
```

Notice that we used two instances of the **JS** plugin:

- The first references a hosted JavaScript file.
- The second includes actual JavaScript code that must be added to the page.

Note *You can use the **JS** plugin to both to add a JavaScript file and to include JavaScript code.*

ENABLING THE JS PLUGIN

In the same way that you had to enable the **HTML** plugin (page 4-45), you must enable the **JS** plugin in order to use it in a wiki page. If you attempt to use a disabled plugin, Tiki displays the following message:

FIGURE 4.45 *Disabled **JS** plugin*

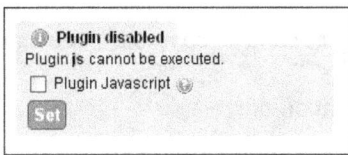

Click **Set** to enable the plugin.

APPROVING THE JS PLUGIN

In the same way that you had to approve the **HTML** plugin (page 4-46), you must approve the **JS** plugin.

1. Click **View Details**. Tiki displays the details of the JS plugin.

FIGURE 4.46 *Details of the **JS** plugin*

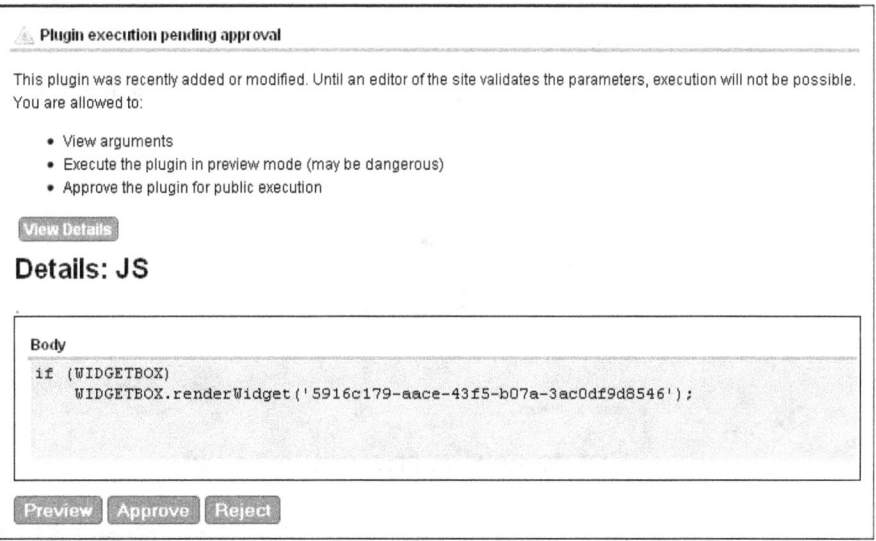

2. Select one of the following options:
    *   Click **Preview** to execute the plugin once. Tiki reloads the page and executes the plugin. But on subsequent page visits, the plugin will not execute.
    *   Click **Approve** to make the plugin "live." Tiki reloads the page, fully executing the plugin code.
    *   Click **Reject** to disapprove the plugin and deny its execution. You should edit the page and remove the denied plugin code.
3. Repeat this procedure for the second **JS** plugin. Remember, the Widgetbox code included *two* scripts (see page 4-48).

Using modules

Modules can add content to your Tiki. Normally, they appear in the left and right columns, but with the **Module** *plugin*, you can add a Tiki module to anything that accepts wiki syntax (such as a wiki page or the **Look and Feel custom code** areas).

Note   *Refer to* **http://doc.tiki.org/Module** *for complete information on Tiki modules*

This section includes information on:

- creating user modules
- assigning modules
- understanding module parameters

CREATING USER MODULES

Tiki *user* modules are created from within the Tiki Admin interface.

Note   *You can also create a custom module by writing the necessary PHP file and its associated TPL template. If you create this type of custom module, please consider contributing your custom module to the Tiki code base.*

To create a user module:

1. From the **Admin: Modules** page, click the **User Modules** tab.

FIGURE 4.47   *Displaying user modules*

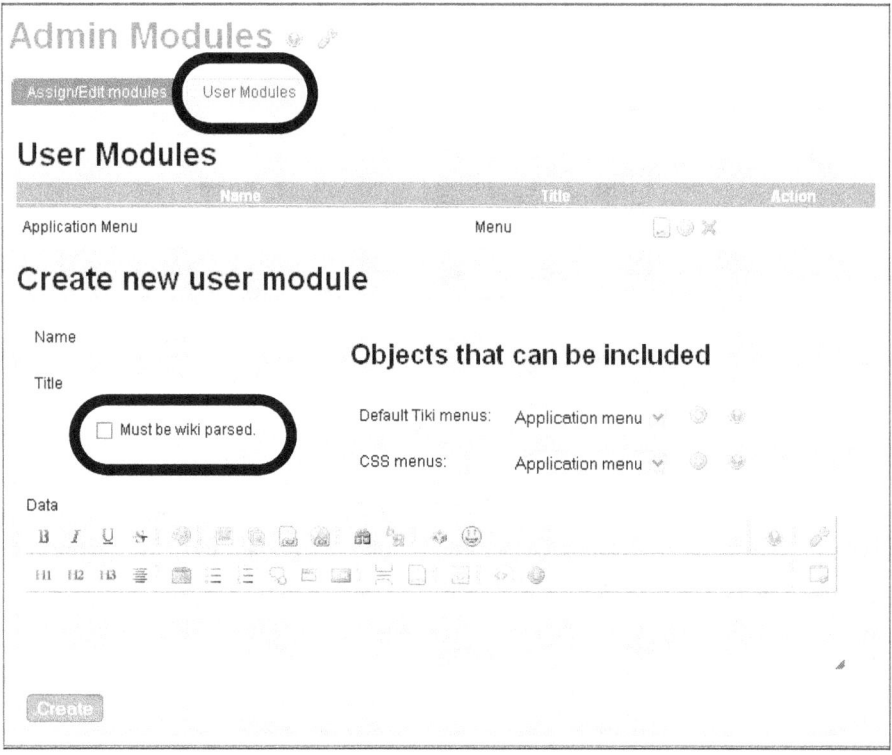

Tiki Essentials

The **User Modules** area lists your existing user modules.

Tip *By default, a new Tiki installation contains a single user module—the **Application Menu**.*

2. Use the **Create new user module** area to create your user module.

Note *To use Tiki's wiki syntax in your module (including embedding modules and plugins) you must choose the **Must be wiki parsed** option.*

3. In the **Data** field, enter the content to appear in the module. This could be text, images, a widget, or anything you want.

For example, to add this weather widget (from **http://weather.com**):

FIGURE 4.48 *Widget from weather.com*

Weather.com generates this code:

Weather.com script

```
<script type="text/javascript" src="http://voap.weather.com/weather/oap/
USDC0001?template=GENXV&par=3000000007&unit=0&key=twciweatherwidget"></script>
```

Remember, Tiki will sanitize any scripts. You'll need to use the **JS** Plugin, as shown on page 4-48:

```
{JS(file="http://voap.weather.com/weather/oap/
USDC0001?template=EVNTV&par=3000000007&unit=0&key=twciweatherwidget") /}
```

4. You can add additional text in the module, as needed.

Your user module

```
Here's the weather where __I__ live.
{JS(file="http://voap.weather.com/weather/oap/
USDC0001?template=EVNTV&par=3000000007&unit=0&key=twciweatherwidget") /}
[http://www.weather.com/|Click here] to find ''your'' local weather report.
```

Tip *Use the **Objects that can be included** area to easily add other Tiki content (such as polls or menus) to the module. Simply select the item to add and click **Add** .*

5. Save the module.

Adding {literal} tags

To include Smarty syntax or code in a module, you must use the **{literal}** tag. For example, you could edit the user module you created to include a personal message for users:

Your user module

```
{literal}{if $user}Hello {$user}!{/if}{/literal}
Here's the weather where __I__ live.
{JS(file="http://voap.weather.com/weather/oap/
USDC0001?template=EVNTV&par=3000000007&unit=0&key=twciweatherwidget") /}
[http://www.weather.com/|Click here] to find ''your'' local weather report.
```

You will also need the **{literal}** to safely use any HTML tags that would otherwise be sanitized by Tiki.

Tip *You could also use the **HTML** plugin to include scripts and embedded HTML tags in your module.*

Warning *If your code is invalid, you may "crash" your site, making your Tiki inaccessible. You will need to edit the module code directly from the database. For more information, see "Fixing modules" on page 106.*

ASSIGNING MODULES

After creating user modules, assign them to the left or right column so that users can interact with them.

Note *You can also add modules to a wiki page by using the **Module** wiki plugin. See ☞ **http://doc.tiki.org/pluginModule** for details.*

For example, to add the module that you created earlier:

1. From the **Admin: Modules** page, click the **User Modules** tab.

FIGURE 4.49 *Displaying your new user module*

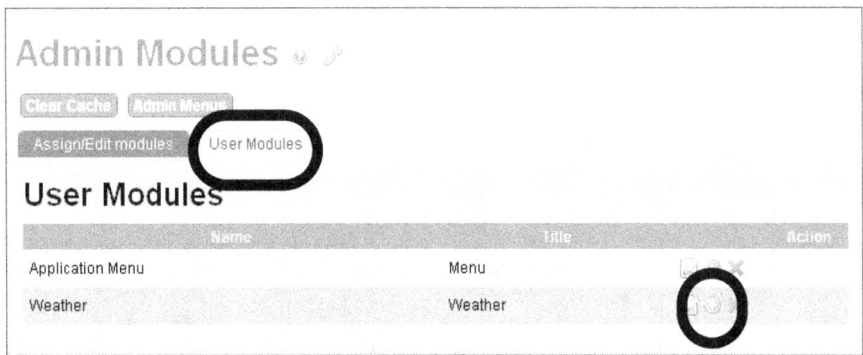

2. Click **Add** ☞ for the module to add to a column.

FIGURE 4.50 *Adding a user module*

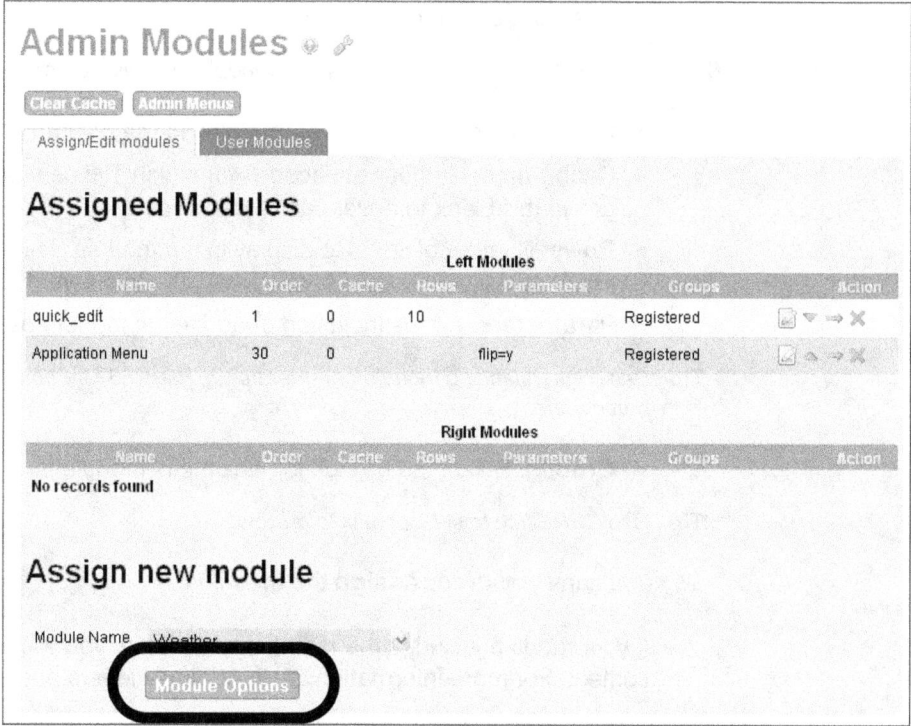

3. On the **Assign/Edit Modules** tab, in the **Assign New Module** area, click **Module Options**.

4. In the **Edit This Assigned Module** area, Tiki:

   • displays a preview of the module.

   • displays the "standard" module parameters.

FIGURE 4.51 *Setting the module options*

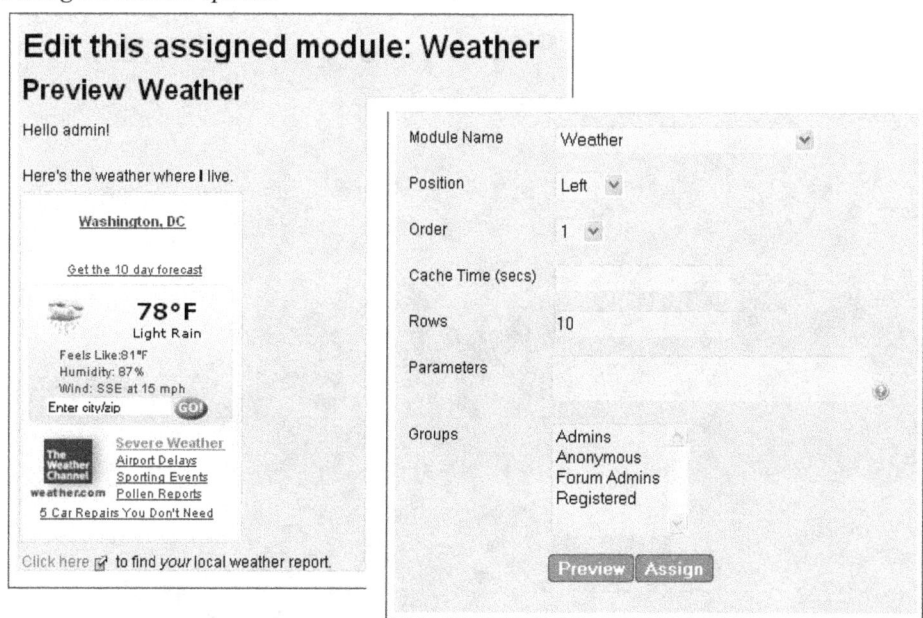

The "standard" options that are available to all modules include:

- **Position**: Left or right column.

Note   *Use the **Module** wiki plugin to add a module to a wiki content page.*

- **Order**: The display order for modules in the column (1= top of column).
- **Cache time**: Number of seconds for which Tiki caches the module contents. Leave this blank to never cache the module.
- **Rows**: Number of items to display in the module. The option applies only when listing specific Tiki objects, such as with the **Newest Blog Post** module.
- **Parameters**: Allows inclusion of additional module parameters.

Tip   *See "Understanding module parameters" on page 55 for information on additional parameters.*

- **Groups**: Select the groups for which this module is visible.

Tip   *Use **Ctrl+Click** to select multiple groups.*

5. You can **Preview** or **Assign** the module.

If your module includes the **HTML** or **JS** plugin, you will need to approve the content. For more information, see "Adding widgets and scripts" on page 42.

UNDERSTANDING MODULE PARAMETERS

You can customize the properties of a module by using its parameters. This section contains information on:

- adding parameters to user modules
- using module-specific parameters

Note *For complete information, refer to* **http://doc.tiki.org/Module+Parameters**.

Adding parameters to user modules
With user modules use the **Parameters** field (when assigning the modules) to apply parameters to the module.

FIGURE 4.52 *Adding parameters to a user module*

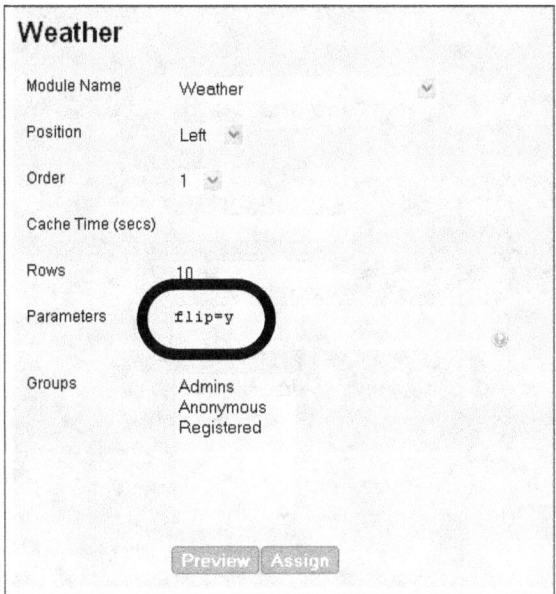

To add multiple parameters, use an ampersand (**&**) to separate the parameters. For example, to specify the following parameters:

- **Flip** = y
- **Nopage** = HomePage

use

```
flip=y&nopage=HomePage
```

Using module-specific parameters

In addition to the standard Tiki module parameters, each module may contain additional parameters specific to that module.

For example, the **Categories** module contains a parameter to specify which category IDs to display in the module.

FIGURE 4.53 *Parameters for the Categories module*

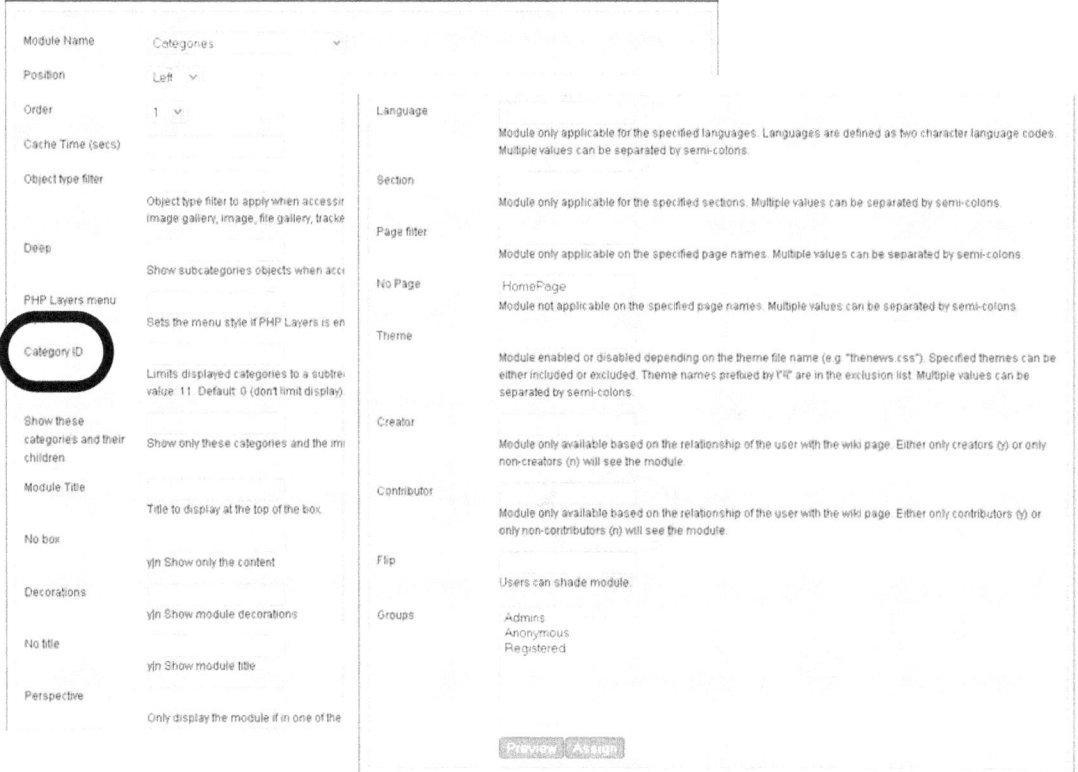

When editing the module, Tiki automatically displays the available parameters for the module.

Note   *For detailed information on each module, see* **http://doc.tiki.org/Module**.

Tiki Essentials

CHAPTER 5   *Writing Your Own Tiki Plugins*

Plugins are one way to extend Tiki's wiki functionality to do anything (and everything) that you want. Although Tiki includes over 100 plugins with its standard installation, you may find it necessary to create your own plugins that meet your specific needs. This chapter will show you how.

IN THIS CHAPTER

When to use a plugin

Basically, you should use a plugin to accomplish anything that you cannot do with regular Tiki wiki syntax. This could be something as simple as changing the font or color of text, or as complex as performing database queries and returning SQL values.

Tip *For complete information on Tiki plugins, see* ☀ ***http://doc.tiki.org/Plugin***.

Of course, you could use existing plugins (such as the HTML or JS plugins) and include the specific code or script. While this method will definitely work (and may even be easier initially), it is not very "future-proof."

If you ever want to change or update the script, you will have to manually make the change everywhere you added it. A plugin can simply be updated once. Tiki will automatically update the code on every page that uses the plugin.

In addition, creating custom plugins allows you to execute PHP code from within the Tiki wiki page. This allows for dynamically generated output.

Note *See "Adding widgets and scripts" on page 42 for additional examples of plugins.*

Writing a simple plugin

This is an example of a pull quote.

Let's write a simple plugin to create a pull quote[1] on a wiki page, as shown on the left side of this page.

We'll want users to be able to define:

- where the pull quote appears (on the left or right side of the page)
- the width (in pixels)
- the color of the text

To begin, create a new, empty PHP file named **wikiplugin_pullquote.php**.

Note *Wiki plugins should be named using the convention:* ***wikiplugin_NAME_OF_THE_PLUGIN.php***.

Note *This section is not a guide to PHP programming. For details on PHP, see* ***http://www.php.net***.

Plugins are created in three basic steps:

1. Entering variables
2. Adding security and help
3. Displaying the output

---

1. A pull quote (also known as a lift-out quote or a call-out) is a quotation or edited excerpt usually placed in a larger typeface on the same page. *Source*: http://en.wikipedia.org/wiki/Pull_quote

Entering variables

In the first portion of our **Pullquote** plugin, you must define the variables that can be used in the plugin. In this example, there are three variables—two optional and one required:

- the text color – optional
- the overall width – optional
- the position (left or right) – required

In this section you'll learn about:

- defining the function
- reading the variables and setting defaults
- error handling

DEFINING THE FUNCTION

The first thing to do is to write the PHP code that defines the **Pullquote** function:

The function

```
function wikiplugin_pullquote($data, $params) {

    $quote = '';

}
```

The name of the function must be in the format **wikiplugin_NAME OF YOUR PLUGIN**. You can name your plugin anything you want—but do not include any spaces. The name used here is that of the plugin that users editing the wiki will use.

In this example, the plugin will be named **_pullquote_**. Therefore, the syntax to use it in a wiki page is: **{PULLQUOTE()}...{PULLQUOTE}** .

Tiki will extract the plugin as:

- $data – the text of the pull quote
- $params – the parameters used in the plugin.
  For more information, see "Reading the variables and setting defaults" on page 60.

The second line (**$quote = '';**) tells Tiki to set the quote (defined by the **$quote** variable) empty, to ensure that we start with an empty variable.

READING THE VARIABLES AND SETTING DEFAULTS

Now that the function has been defined, we can read in the three variables. In this example, we define the variables as:

- **$color** – the text color
- **$width** – the overall width of the pullquote
- **$float** – which side (left or right) of the page

In this example, we'll set the color of the text:

Setting the color

```
if (!isset($color))
    {
// Set default color
        $c = '#000000';
    } else {
        $c = '#'.$color;
    }
```

Notice that first we check to see that the user specified a color. Remember, the color is optional; it may not be included. If the user did not include a color code, the plugin defaults to **#000000** (black text).

Notice, too, that we added a hash (**#**) to the beginning of the color code. This is important because HTML hex colors codes must start with a # sign. In the plugin help, we need to make sure to tell users not to include the # sign, since the plugin adds it automatically.

We can use similar code to determine the width:

Inputting width

```
if (!isset($width))
    {
// Set default width
        $w = '250px';
    } else {
        $w = $width . 'px';
    }
```

Here, we add **px** to the end of the width. Again, we'll need to make sure that the help tells users not to include the **px** with the width.

If the user did not include a width, the plugin defaults to **250px**.

ERROR HANDLING

The third option, **float** (the position of the pull quote: **left** or **right**), is required. We can add logic to confirm that the user added a position:

Checking for the position

```
if (!isset($float))
    {
// No position, tell the user
        $msg = 'Please select a position: left or right.';
        return $msg;
    } else {
// Set the position
        $f = $float;
    }
```

Now, a user forgetting to enter a position will be reminded.

Finally, we'll confirm that there is actually text to use as the pull quote.

Checking for text

```
if ($data eq '')
    {
// No text, tell user
        $msg = 'Please include text for the pull quote.';
        return $msg;
    }
```

Now, if a user tries to use the plugin without any text (such as **{PULLQUOTE()}...{PULLQUOTE}** or **{PULLQUOTE() /}**) they'll get an error message.

Adding security and help

What good is creating the perfect Tiki plugin if no one knows how to use it?
It is important to always include proper documentation and help for your plugins.
In fact, Tiki will ignore plugins without this information.

First, we'll add help text that appears when users list the available Tiki plugins.

FIGURE 5.54 *The plugin's help text*

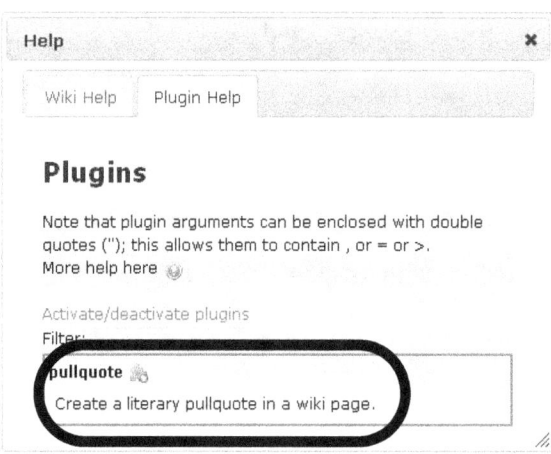

Creating plugin help

```
function wikiplugin_pullquote_help() {
    return tra("Create a literary pullquote").":<br />
~np~{PULLQUOTE(width=###|color=######,
float=left|right)}".tra("text")."{PULLQUOTE}~/np~";
    }
```

Now we'll add detailed help information for the Tiki inline plugin help (when users
add the plugin through the Tiki help interface).

FIGURE 5.55 *The detailed help*

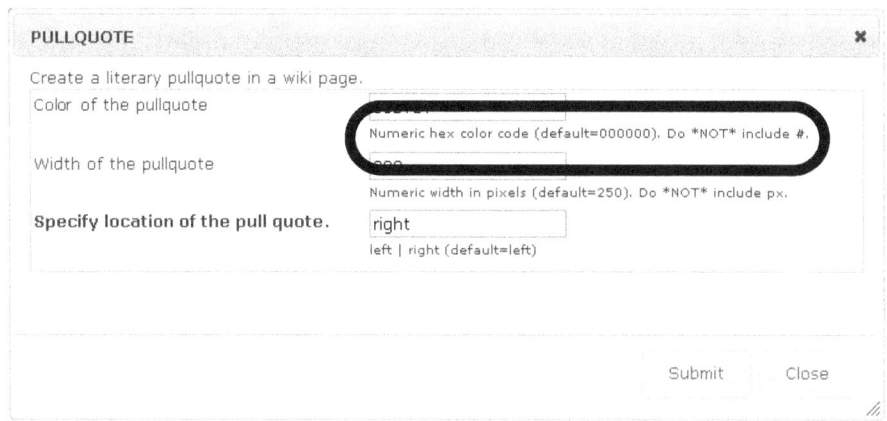

```
function wikiplugin_pullquote_info() {
    return array(
        'name' => tra('Pullquote'),
        'description' => tra('Create a literary pullquote in a wiki page.'),
        'validate' => 'all',
        'params' => array(
            'float' => array(
                'required' => true,
                'name' => tra('Specify location of the pull quote.'),
                'description' => tra('left | right (default=left)'),
                'filter' => 'alpha',
            ),
            'color' => array(
                'required' => false,
                'name' => tra(Color of the pullquote'),
                'description' => tra('Numeric hex color code (default=000000). Do *NOT*
include #.'),
                'filter' => 'alnum',
            ),
            'width' => array(
                'required' => false,
                'name' => tra('Width of the pullquote'),
                'description' => tra('Numeric width in pixels (default=250). Do *NOT*
include px.'),
                'filter' => 'int',
            ),
        ),
    );
}
```

Notice the lines highlighted in the sample code:

- **'validate' => 'all'**: This tells Tiki that a trusted site editor (with the necessary permissions) must validate (that is, approve) the plugin before it becomes active on the page.

- **'required' => true**: The float parameter is required; users must select a position (left or right). Tiki will not allow users to add the plugin to a wiki page without entering this parameter.

Note *Learn more about all the possible plugin variables on* *http://dev.tiki.org/Plugin*.

Displaying the output

Now we're ready to build and display the output: the pull quote. Remember the **$quote** variable that you created previously? Now we need to create it.

Building the quote

```
$quote .= "<div style='float:".$f.";width:".$w."'>";
$quote .= "<div class='pullquote'><div class='content' style='color:".$c.";'>";
$quote .= $data;
$quote .= "</div></div></div>";
```

Warning   *Including HTML output in a plugin may make your Tiki vulnerable to XSS (cross-scripting) attacks. Although this example uses HTML, you should consider using an Smarty template instead. See* **http://dev.tiki.org/Hello+world** *for more information.*

The **$data** variable represents the actual quote text. Remember the error checking from before, to ensure that the text isn't empty?

- The **$f** represents the position.
- The **$w** represents the width.
- The **$c** represents the color.

Tip   *Notice that the text of the pull quote is enclosed in a **<div>** element using the **pullquote** class (*<div class="pullquote">*). This allows you to customize the styling by adding a custom CSS style element (that is, **pullquote**). For example, you could style the quote:*

Sample CSS

```
.pullquote {
    font-family:Times,serif;
    font-size:1.6em;
    font-style:italic;
    font-weight:bold;
    line-height:1em;
    margin:10px;
    padding:20px 10px;
    }
```

For more information, see "Adding custom CSS styles" on page 30.

USING THE PLUGIN

Now that you've built the **Pullquote** plugin, it is time to use it in wiki page.

1. Copy the **wikiplugin_pullquote.php** plugin file to the **.../lib/wiki-plugins/...** directory.

Your plugin should look similar to:

The completed Pullquote plugin

```php
<?php

// Wiki plugin to create a pull quote
// Created as part of Tiki Essentials: http://twessentials.keycontent.org
// By Rick Sapir, Copyright (C) 2010. All rights reserved.
// Licensed under the GNU LESSER GENERAL PUBLIC LICENSE (LGPL).

function wikiplugin_pullquote_help() {
    return tra("Create a literary pullquote")."":<br />
~np~{pullquote(width=###|color=######, float=left|right)}".tra("text")."{pullquote}~/
np~ ";
    }

function wikiplugin_pullquote_info() {
    return array(
        'name' => tra('Pullquote'),
        'description' => tra('Create a literary pullquote in a wiki page.'),
        'validate' => 'all',
        'params' => array(
            'color' => array(
                'required' => false,
                'name' => tra('Code of the pullquote'),
                'description' => tra('Numeric hex color code (default=000000). Do *NOT*
include #.'),
                'filter' => 'alnum',
            ),
            'width' => array(
                'required' => false,
                'name' => tra('Width of the pullquote'),
                'description' => tra('Numeric width in pixels (default=250). Do *NOT*
include px.'),
                'filter' => 'int',
            ),
            'float' => array(
                'required' => true,
                'name' => tra('Specify location of the pull quote.'),
                'description' => tra('left | right (default=left)'),
                'filter' => 'alpha',
            ),

        ),
    );
}
```

```
function wikiplugin_pullquote($data, $params) {

    extract ($params,EXTR_SKIP);

    $quote ='';

// Check for color
    if (!isset($color))
    {
// Set default color
        $c = '#000000';
    } else {
        $c = '#'.$color;
    }

// Check for width
    if (!isset($width))
    {
// Set default width
        $w= '250px';
    } else {
        $w = $width . 'px';
    }

// Check for position
if (!isset($float))
    {
// No position, tell the user
        $msg = 'Please select a position: left or right.';
        return $msg;
    } else {
// Set the position
        $f = $float;
    }

//Build the output
    $quote .= "<div style='float:".$f.";width:".$w."'>";
    $quote .= "<div class='pullquote'><div class='content' style='color:".$c.";'>";
    $quote .= $data;
    $quote .= "</div></div></div>";

    return $quote;
}

?>
```

2. Add your newly created plugin to a wiki page.

FIGURE 5.56 *Adding the Pullquote plugin to a wiki page*

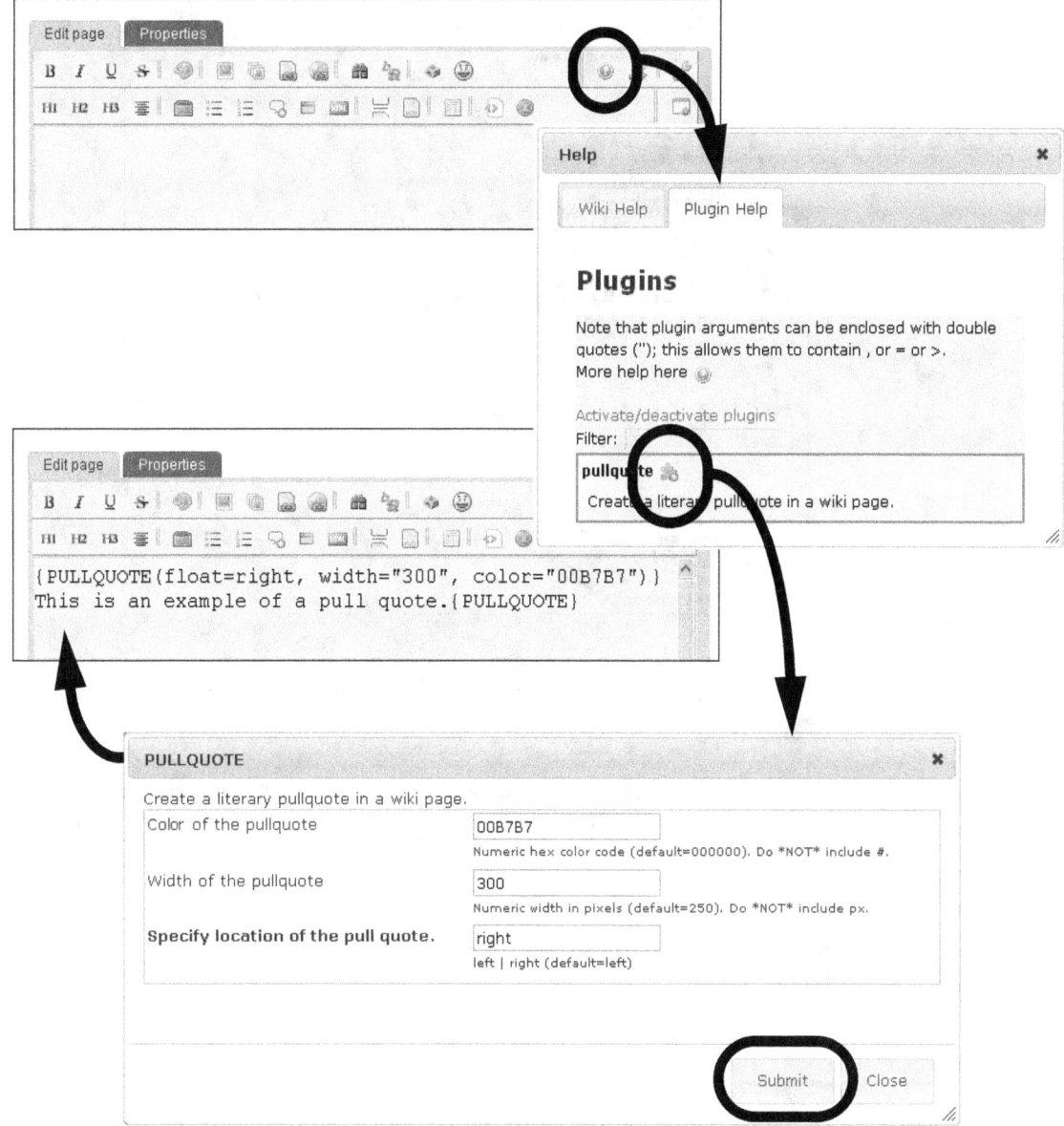

3. If the plugin requires approval (if you specified the security), use the **Plugin Approval** page to approve it.

FIGURE 5.57 *Approving the Pullquote plugin*

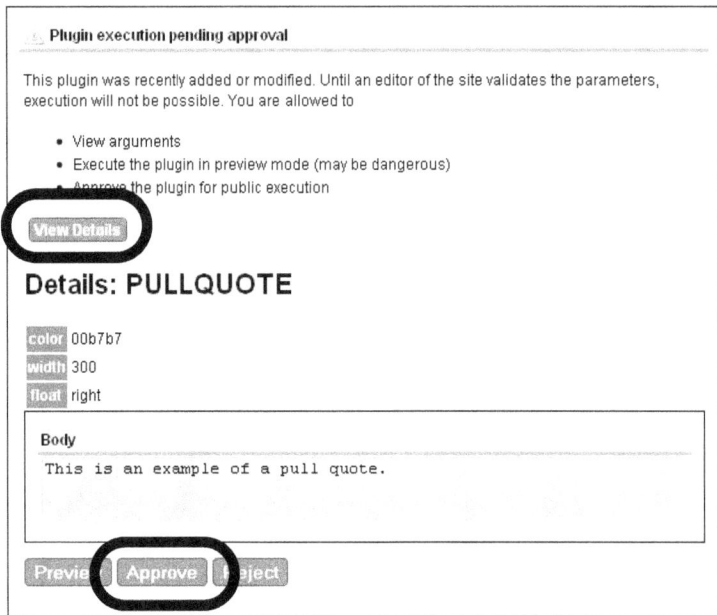

The process is identical to "Approving the HTML plugin" on page 46, or "Approving the JS plugin" on page 49.

If you create useful plugins, please consider contributing them to the Tiki community. It is quick and easy. See "Joining the Tiki Community" on page 109 to learn how.

CHAPTER 6

Using Tiki Profiles to Configure your Site

A Tiki **profile** is a set of configurations that can be applied to your site. Since Tiki contains hundreds of features, preferences, modules, and permissions, using a profile is an easy way to configure multiple features in a single process.

FIGURE 6.58   *Tiki Profiles make it easy to configure your site.*

Applying a profile to your site does not erase your data. This means you can apply profiles to your site at any time. Profiles can even be applied "on top of" one another. You can even create your own profile!

The Tiki Profiles site has a number of profiles available to ease your Tiki customization. See **http://profiles.tiki.org** for details.

IN THIS CHAPTER

Using profile repositories

Profiles are stored in a *repository*. The Tiki Community maintains a community profile repository. You can also create your own repository.

In this section, you'll learn about:

- accessing the Tiki repository
- creating your own repository

ACCESSING THE TIKI REPOSITORY

To configure your site to access the Tiki repository:

Note *The Tiki repository is normally configured, by default, for all new Tiki installations.*

1. On the **Admin: Profiles** page, at the **Advanced** tab, in the **Repository URL** field, add **http://profiles.tiki.org/profiles**.

FIGURE 6.59 *Adding the Tiki Profile repository*

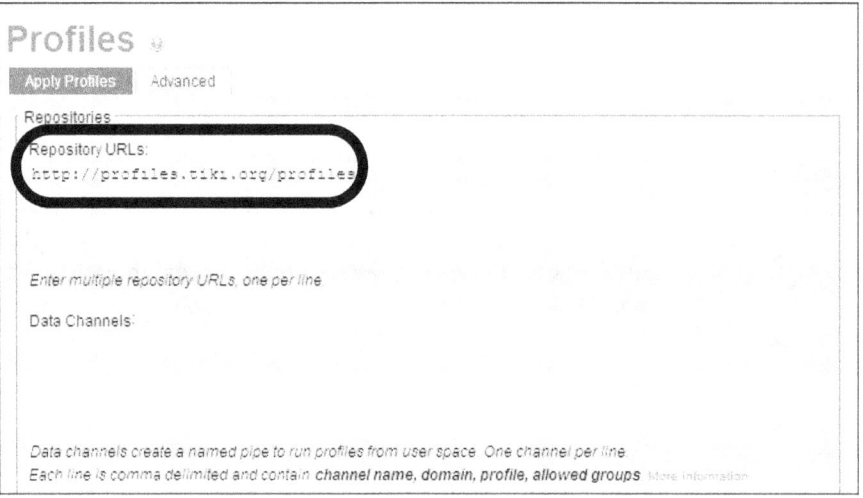

2. Click **Save**.

To confirm that Tiki can access the Tiki repository, review the **Status** area of the **Apply Profiles** tab.

FIGURE 6.60 *Confirming that Tiki can contact the repository*

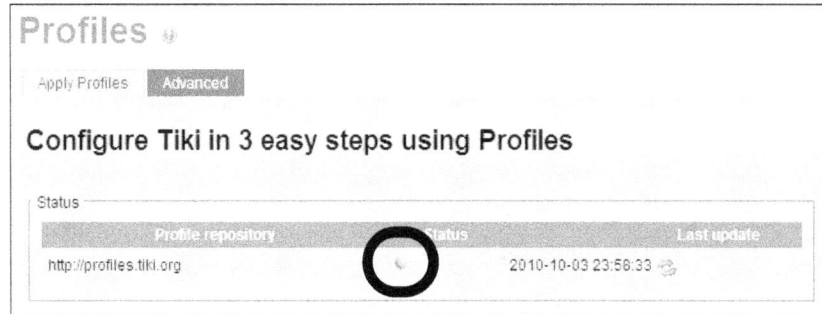

3. Click **Refresh** .

4. Verify that the repository **Status** is (connected). You can now apply profiles from the repository.

Note *If your site requires a proxy to access the internet, confirm that the settings are correct on the **Admin: General** page.*

CREATING YOUR OWN REPOSITORY

If you are unable to connect to the Tiki Community repository (for example, if you are behind a corporate firewall) you can easily create your own local repository. It is as simple as installing a Tiki site and making a few, simple changes:

1. Create a category for the profiles (for example, **My Profiles**).

Note *For information about Tiki Categories, see **http://doc.tiki.org/Category**.*

2. Assign the following permissions to the Anonymous group:
   - **tiki_p_view**
   - **tiki_p_export_wiki**
   - **tiki_p_view_category**

Note *For information on Tiki Permissions, see **http://doc.tiki.org/Permissions**.*

3. Assign the profiles to the category you created in **Step 1**. Now the site can be used as a Profiles Repository for other sites.

   For additional information, see **http://profiles.tiki.org**.

Tip *You can use the **Repository Profile** to easily turn your Tiki into a repository.*

Applying profiles

To apply a profile, your Tiki must have access to the profile repository. You can obtain profiles from the Tiki Community profile repository, or create your own.

To apply a profile:

1. From the Administration page, click **Profiles**.
2. On the **Profiles** page, click the **Apply Profiles** tab.

Tip *Use the **Advanced** tab to configure additional profile repositories and data channels.*

3. Click **Featured Profiles** to display a list of popular profiles.

FIGURE 6.61 *Selecting a profile to apply*

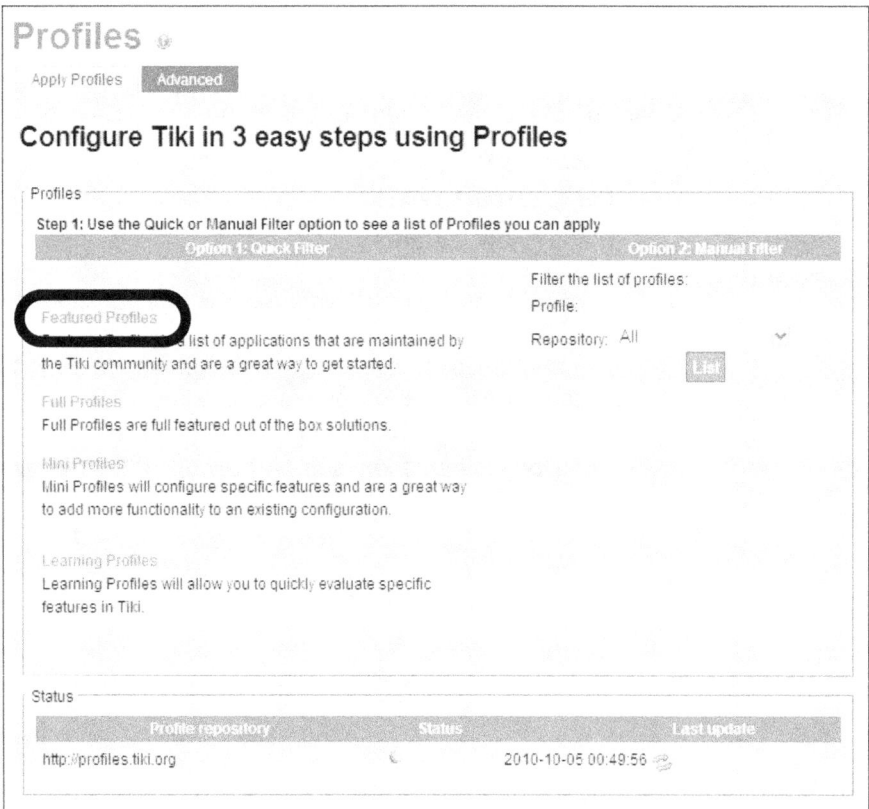

Tiki offers additional lists of profiles (**Full**, **Mini**, and **Learning**) as well as customizable filters to help you select a profile.

4. Tiki contacts the profiles repository and displays the profiles that match your filter.

If Tiki is unable to contact the repository:

- Test your connection. In the **Status** area, and click **Refresh** ♻. Tiki will attempt to contact the repository.
- Check the **Repository URL**. On the **Advanced** tab, confirm that the **Repository URL** is correct.

FIGURE 6.62 *The available profiles, based on selected filters*

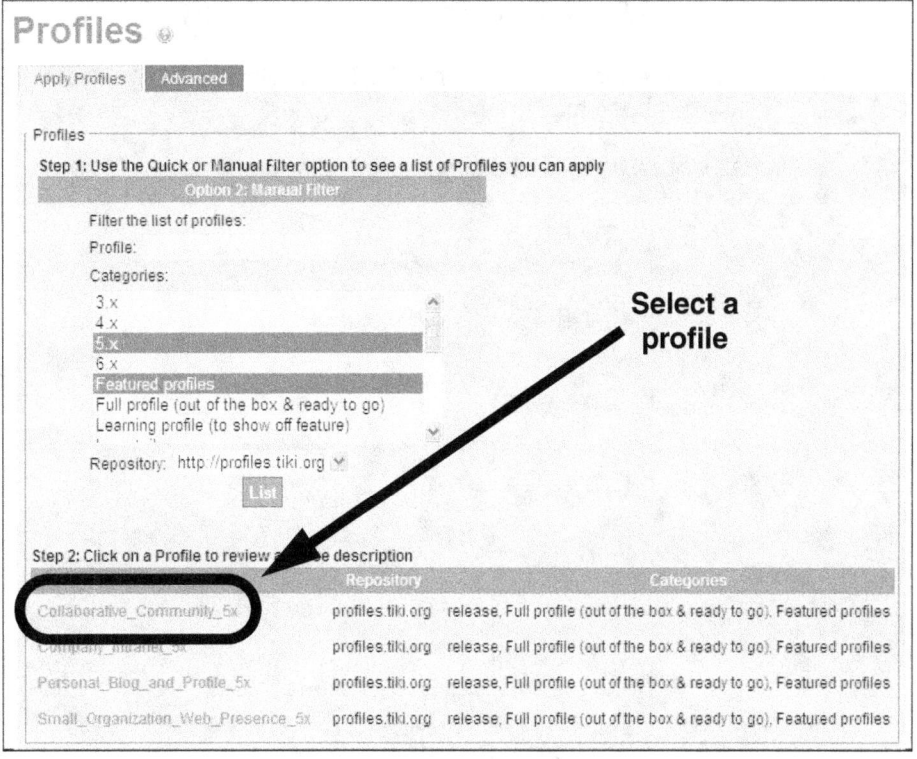

5. Click a profile name. Tiki displays the release information for the selected profile.

FIGURE 6.63 *Selected profile*

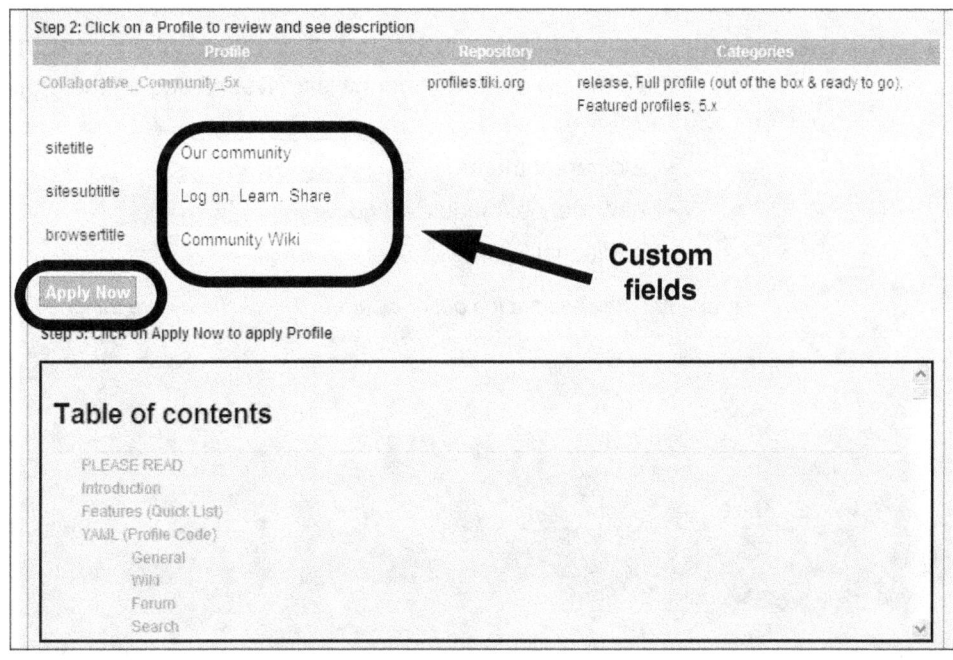

Some profiles allow you to customize the installation. For example, you can configure the **Name** or **Title** of your site.

6. Read the profile information and click **Apply Now** to apply the profile to your site.

7. Tiki prompts for confirmation before applying the profile. Click **OK**.

After applying the profile, Tiki displays a list of all configuration changes that have been made.

FIGURE 6.64 *Tiki shows the changes made by the profile.*

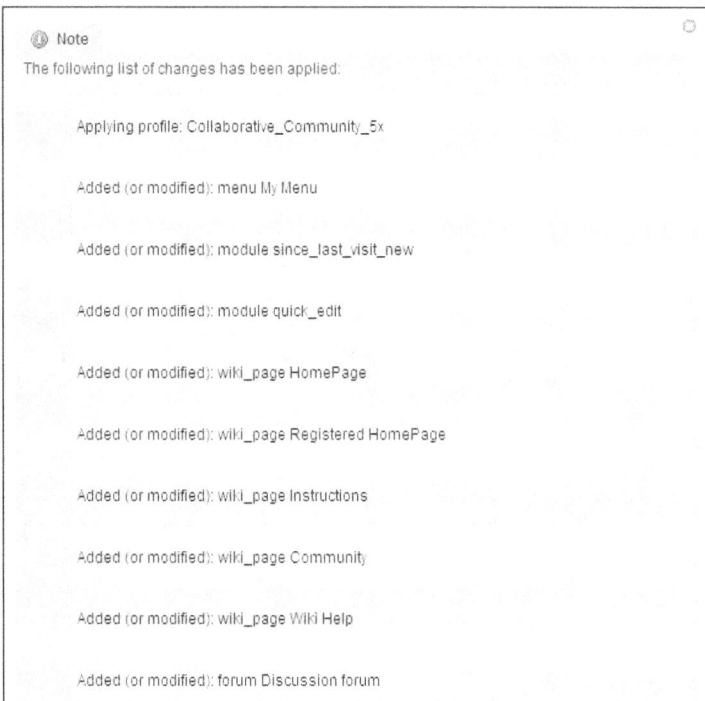

You can now explore your new site. Depending on the profile you selected, you may notice:

- a different theme
- new menus, modules, and pages
- additional features

Note *You may need to log out or clear the Tiki cache before the changes take affect.*

CHAPTER 7

Using Trackers to Collect and Display User Information

A Tiki **tracker** is a way to collect, store, and organize data. You might think of a tracker as a mini database or spreadsheet that runs inside your Tiki site. Trackers are also especially useful for creating forms that your site's visitors can complete.

When using trackers, Tiki will create the necessary HTML form elements and record the results.

IN THIS CHAPTER

Building forms

In this section, we'll create a simple form (a tracker) to collect information from website users.

In their simplest format, the steps to build a form from a tracker are:

1. Creating a tracker
2. Entering the tracker data
3. Displaying the tracker data

Note *The sample tracker that you will create in this section is also used in the "Using dynamic lists" and "Creating pretty trackers" sections, later in this chapter.*

ENABLING TRACKERS

To create a Tracker, first enable the **Tracker** feature on the **Admin: Features** page.

FIGURE 7.65 *Enabling trackers*

Now you're ready to create the tracker.

CREATING A TRACKER

To create a new tracker:

1. From the **Admin** menu, select **Trackers > Admin Trackers**.
2. Click the **Create Tracker** tab.

FIGURE 7.66 *Creating a tracker to maintain visitor information*

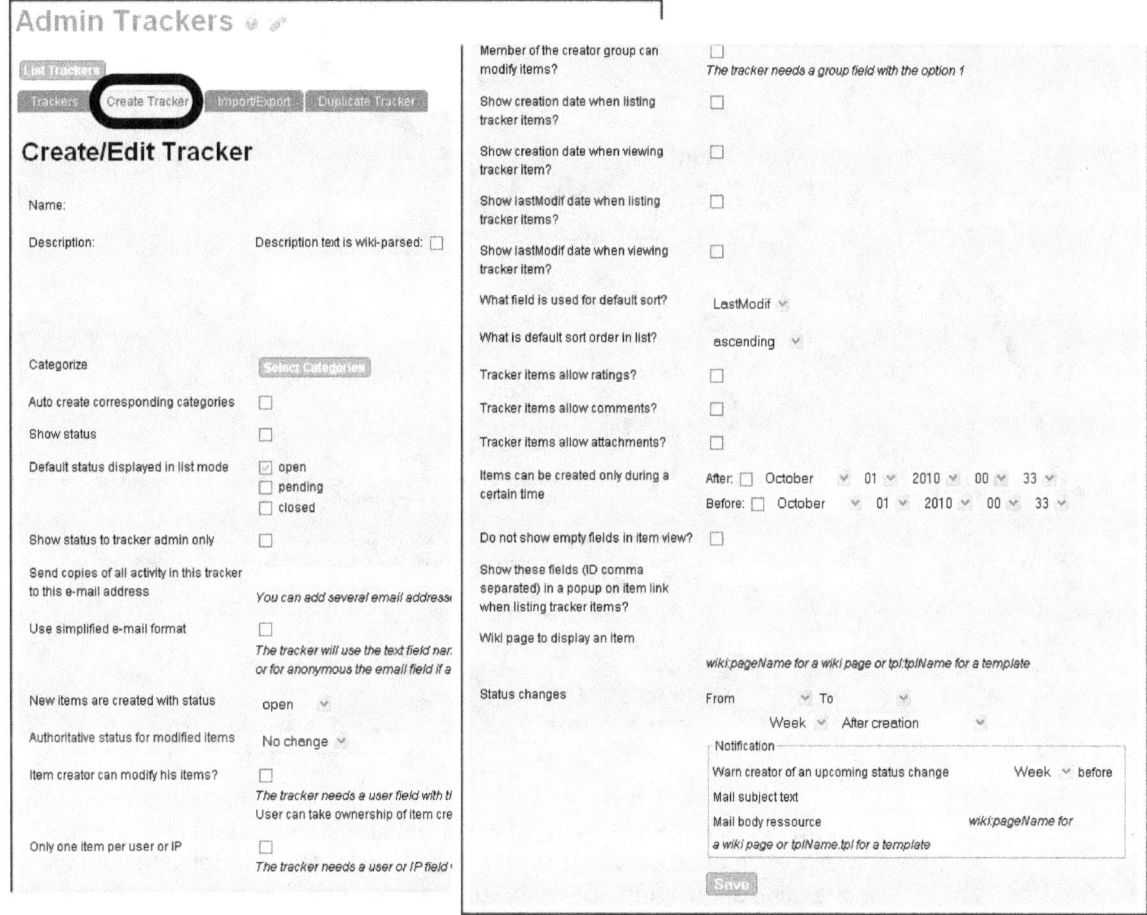

3. On the **Create/Edit Tracker** tab, complete the following fields:

- **Name**: Name of the tracker.

- **Description**: Brief description of the tracker. Enable the **Description text is wiki-parsed** option to format the description with wiki syntax.

- **Show status**: Specifies whether the tracker shows (or uses) a status field. For example, if you are using a Tracker for a bug reporting system, you may need to set the status of each bug.

  You can also specify whether items of a particular status are shown when listing a tracker, whether the status is visible only to the Admin, and the default status of newly created items.

Note *There is a difference between* listing *and* viewing *trackers: When listing, Tiki displays the tracker items in a table; when you view, Tiki displays each tracker item on a separate page, as shown in Figure 7.67 on page 78.*

FIGURE 7.67   *The difference between* listing *and* viewing *tracker items*

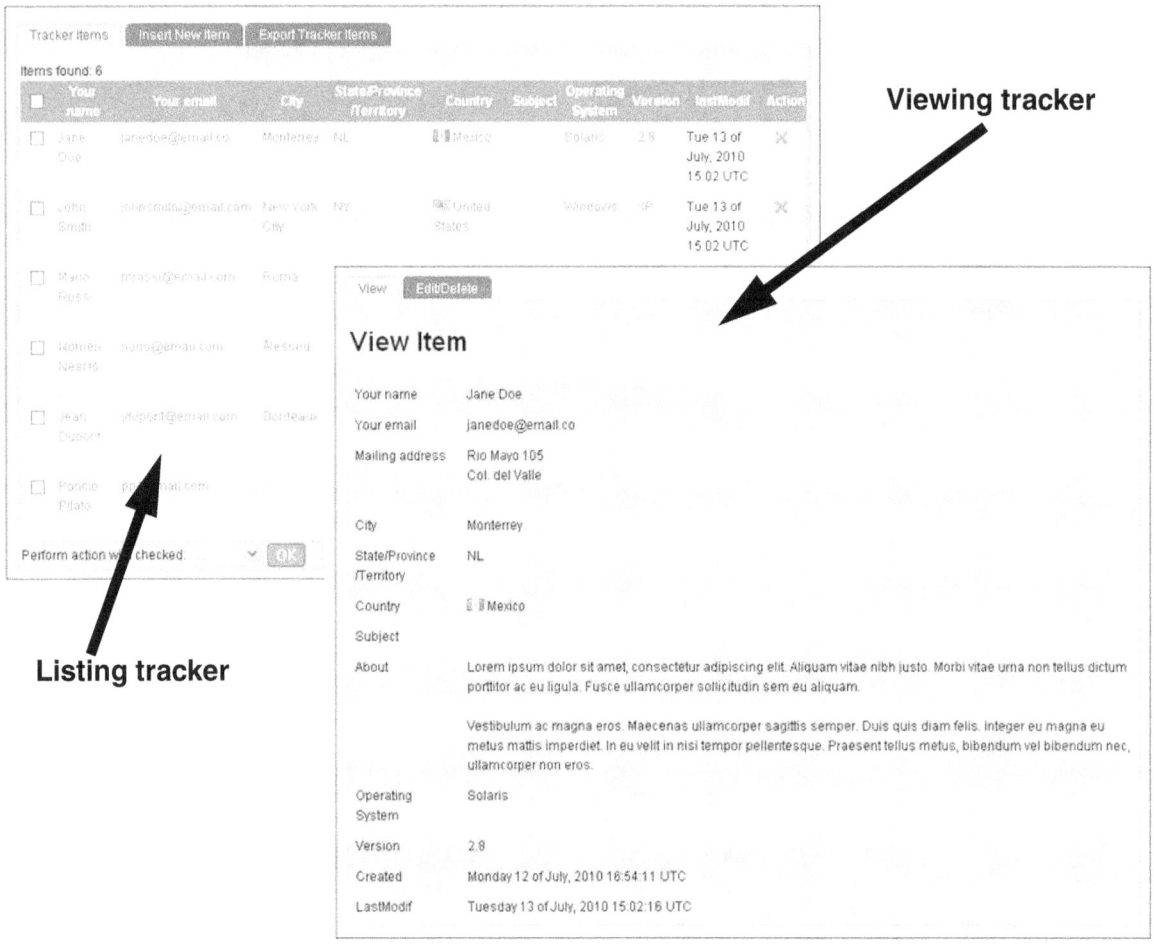

- **Send copies of all activity…**: Enter email addresses that are to receive notification of all activity (creating new items, editing or deleting items, changing status, and so on) for this tracker.

  You can also specify whether the email is sent in a simplified format. By default the notification message *will not* include any tracker details. Enable the **Use simplified e-mail format** field to override this.

- **Show date…** fields: Specify if the creation and last modified dates are shown when *listing* and *viewing* the tracker. You can also override the site's default date and time formats.

- **Default sort…** fields: Select the field to use as the default sort field (and its order) when listing tracker items. Since you have not added any tracker fields yet, you can only select the *creation* and *last modified* dates.

4. Click **Save**. Tiki saves the tracker.

5. Click the **Trackers** tab to display the newly created tracker.

FIGURE 7.68 *The newly created tracker*

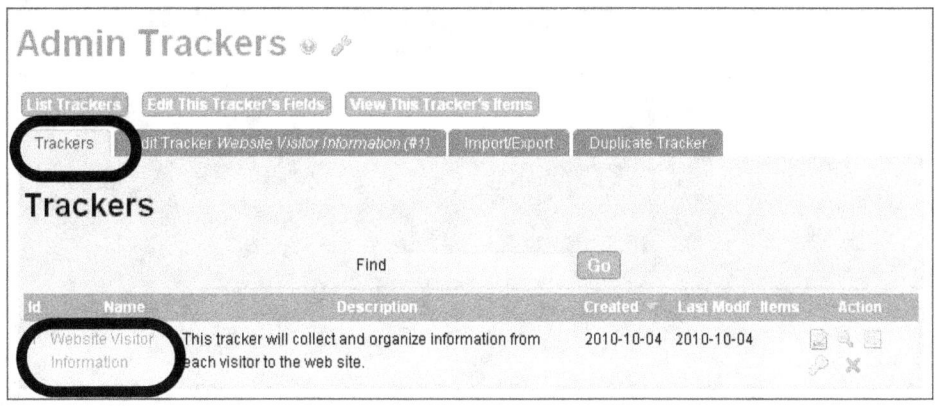

Tip *Be sure to note the ID of the tracker; you'll need it later.*

CREATING TRACKER FIELDS

Now that you have an "empty" tracker, you need to create fields for the tracker. These fields represent the form fields that visitors will complete.

1. From the **Admin: Trackers** page, click **Fields** ▦ for the tracker you created.

FIGURE 7.69 *Adding fields to a tracker*

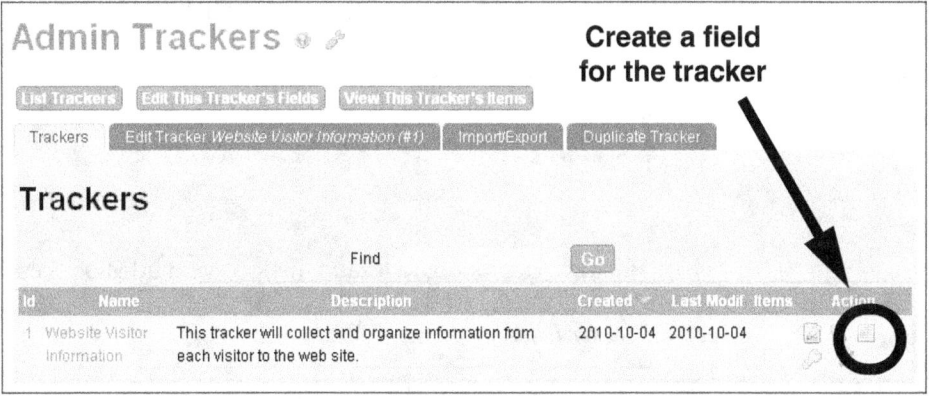

2. On the **Admin: Tracker** page, click the **New Tracker Field** tab.

FIGURE 7.70   *Adding a tracker field*

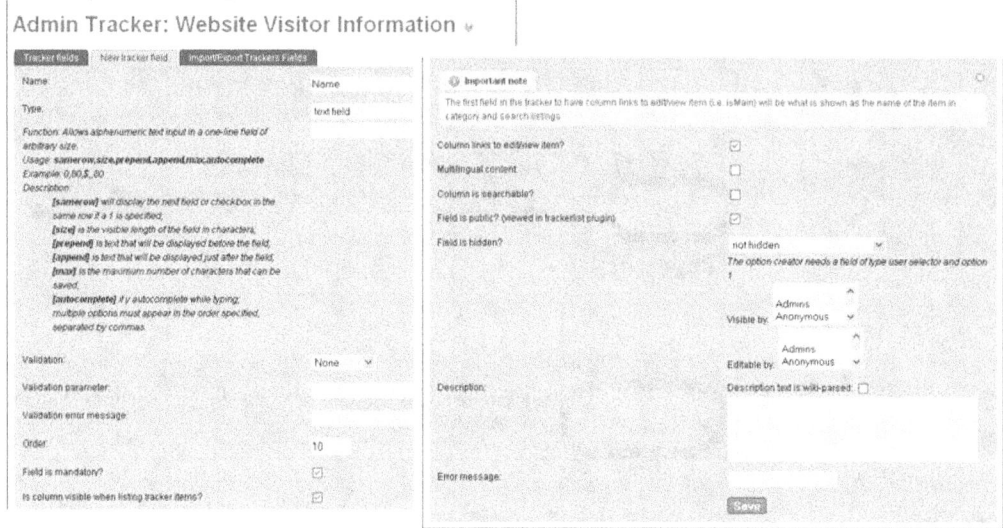

3. Enter the following information in each field on the page:
   - **Name**: Name
     This is the label for the field, as it will appear on the form.
   - **Type**: textfield
   - **Field is mandatory?**: Enable this field.
     This will require all visitors to complete the **Name** field.

   Leave the other fields as their defaults.

4. Click **Save**. Tiki adds the field to the tracker.

FIGURE 7.71   *The new tracker field*

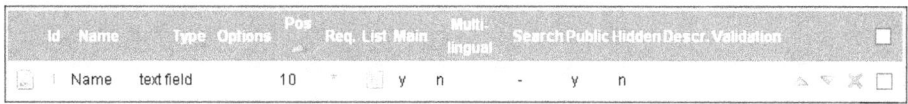

Repeat this procedure to add the following additional tracker fields:

TABLE 7.1   *Tracker fields*

Field	Type	Options
Email	email	Mandatory
Address	textarea	
City	textfield	
State/Province	textfield	
Country	country selector	Mandatory
About	text area	
Subject[a]	textfield	

a. If you selected the **Use simplified email format** option when creating the tracker (see Figure 7.66 on page 77), you must create this **Subject** field.

FIGURE 7.72 *The completed fields for the tracker*

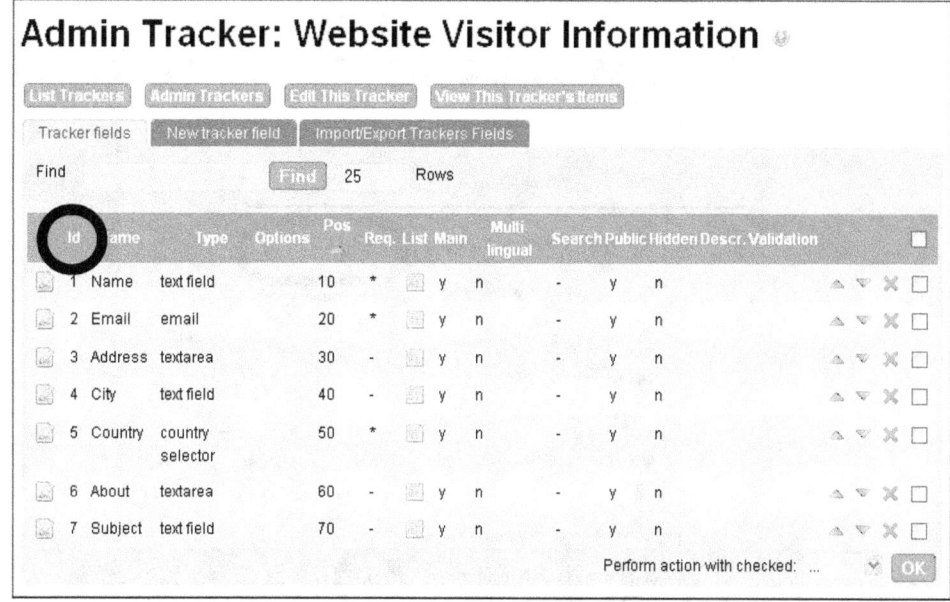

Tip *Be sure to note the ID for each tracker field; you'll need them later.*

FINALIZING THE TRACKER

Now that all fields have been added to the tracker, we can complete the remaining options for the tracker.

1. Click the **Edit this Tracker** button.

FIGURE 7.73 *Return to the Edit Tracker page.*

2. Make the following changes:

FIGURE 7.74 *Updating the tracker*

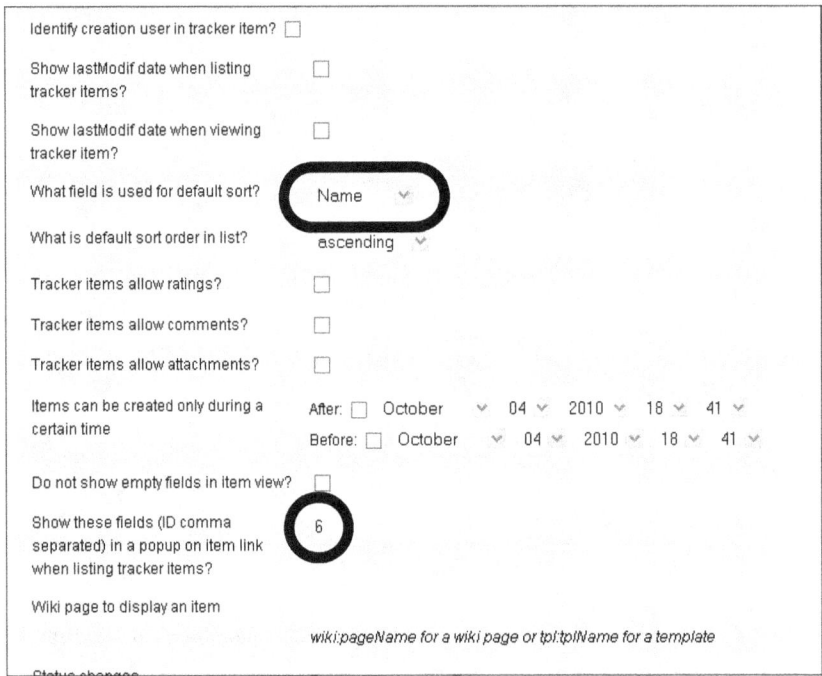

- **What field is used for default sort?**: Select **Name**.
  All tracker items will now be sorted by the user's *name*.

- **Show these fields in a popup...**: Enter the field ID that corresponds to the **About** field. See Figure 7.72 on page 81.

3. Click **Save**.

Entering tracker data

The easiest (and most common) method to enter tracker data is to use the **Tracker** plugin to create a form. An alternative method, is to enter tracker data directly from the Tracker interface pages.

One advantage of using the **Tracker** plugin is that it allows you to add the form to any wiki page, thereby giving you more control over the display of the form.

To create a tracker form:

1. Create a new wiki page.
2. In the wiki page, enter the following:

Tracker plugin

```
{TRACKER(trackerId="TRACKER_ID", fields="FIELD:FIELD:FIELD:…",
showtitle="n", showdesc="y", showmandatory="y", reset="Clear",
submit="Send")}Thank you{TRACKER}
```

where

- **TRACKER_ID** = The ID of the tracker that you created. See Figure 7.68 on page 79.
- **FIELD** = The ID number of each tracker field that you created. See Figure 7.72 on page 81.
  If you created a **Subject** field, *do not* include it here.

Note *The other parameters tell Tiki:*
*- not to display the name of the tracker (**showtitie="n"**)*
*- to display the description of the tracker (**showdesc="y"**)*
*- to indicate which fields users must be completed (**showmandatory="y"**)*
*- to include a reset button (that will erase the form) labeled **Clear** (**reset="Clear"**)*
*- to include a submit button (that will send the form) labeled **Send** (**submit="Send"**)*

FIGURE 7.75   *Adding the Tracker plugin to a wiki page*

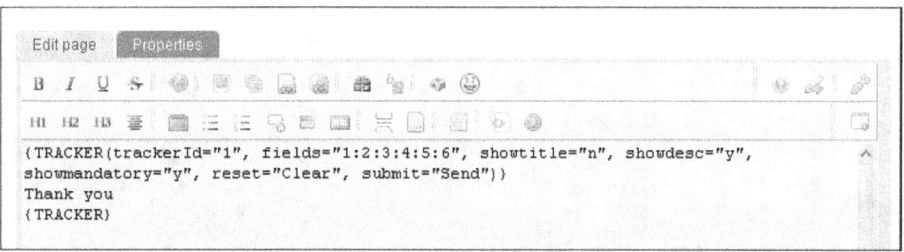

Tip *See ⭐ **http://doc.tiki.org/Plugin** for complete information on the available plugin parameters.*

Note *Be sure to use the tracker field ID and not the order. The actual order in which you include the fields in the **Tracker** plugin is unimportant. Tiki uses the **Order** field that was specified when creating the tracker fields. See Figure 7.72 on page 81.*

Alternatively, you can use the Tiki Help to add the **Tracker** plugin to the wiki page.

FIGURE 7.76 *Using the Plugin Help to add the necessary parameters*

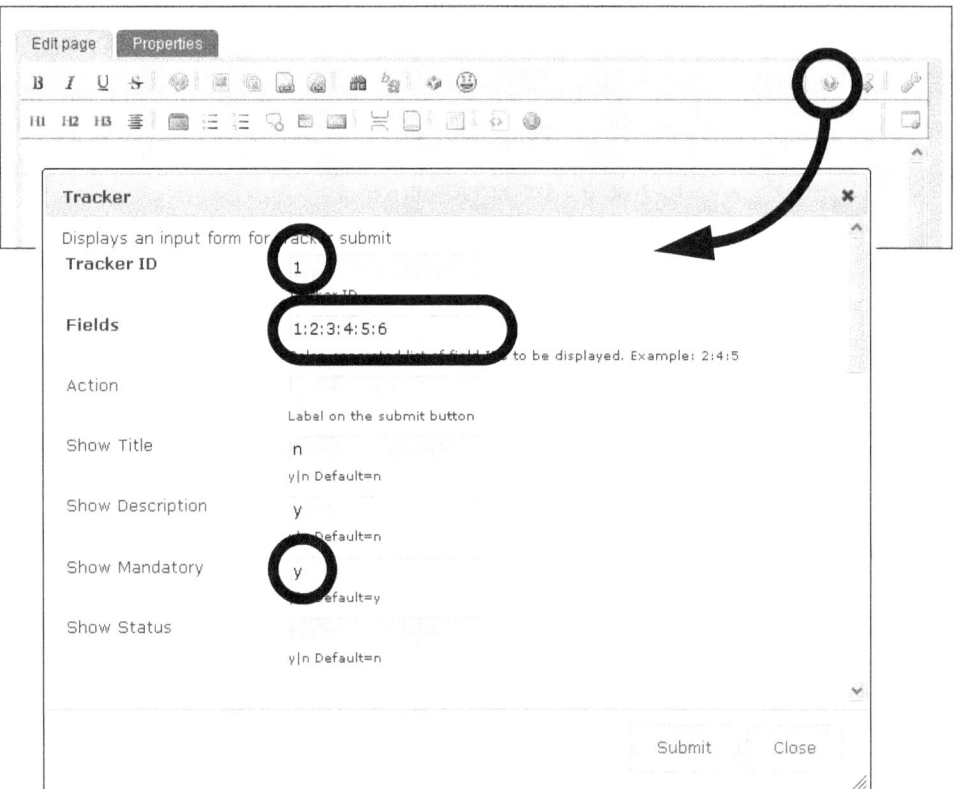

3. Save the wiki page.
4. You can now use the form to enter tracker items. Add several items, using the newly created form.

FIGURE 7.77 *The Tracker plugin displays the tracker as a Web form on a wiki page.*

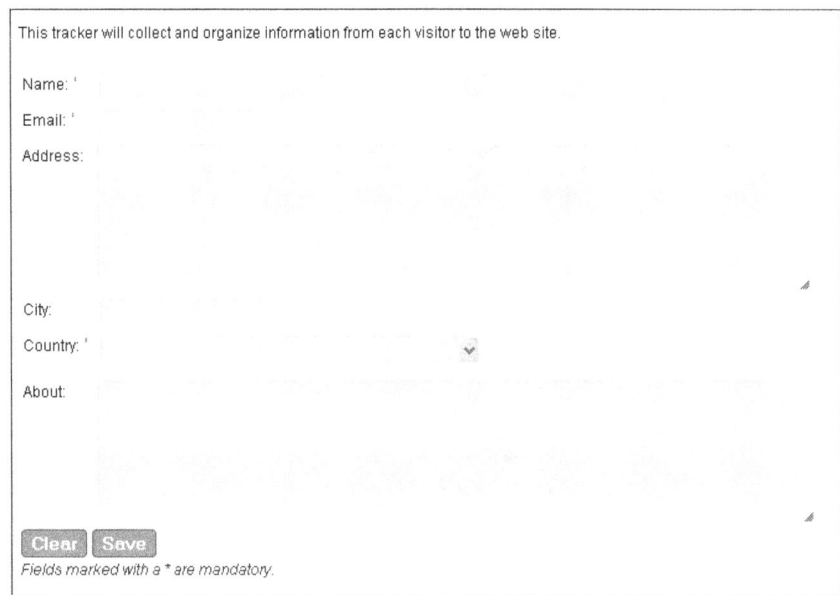

Displaying tracker data

The easiest (and most common) way to display tracker data is to use the **Trackerlist** plugin to create a table with the form data. An alternative method, is to display tracker data on the Tracker interface pages.

One advantage of using the Trackerlist plugin is that it allows you to add the form to any wiki page, thereby giving you more control over the display of the form.

To create a table:

1. Create a new wiki page.
2. In the wiki page, enter the following:

Trackerlist plugin

```
{trackerlist trackerId="TRACKER_ID", fields="FIELD:FIELD:FIELD",
popup="POPUP_FIELD", showtitle="y", showlinks="y", shownbitems="y",
showcreated="y", showfieldname="y", showrss="y"}
```

where

- **TRACKER_ID** = The ID of the tracker that you created. See Figure 7.68 on page 79.

- **FIELD** = The ID numbers of the **Name**, **Email**, and **Country** tracker fields that you created. See Figure 7.68 on page 79.

- **POPUPFIELD** = The ID number of the **About** tracker field. The user's "about" information will display in a pop-up window. See Figure 7.79 on page 86.

FIGURE 7.78   *Adding the Tracker List plugin to a wiki page*

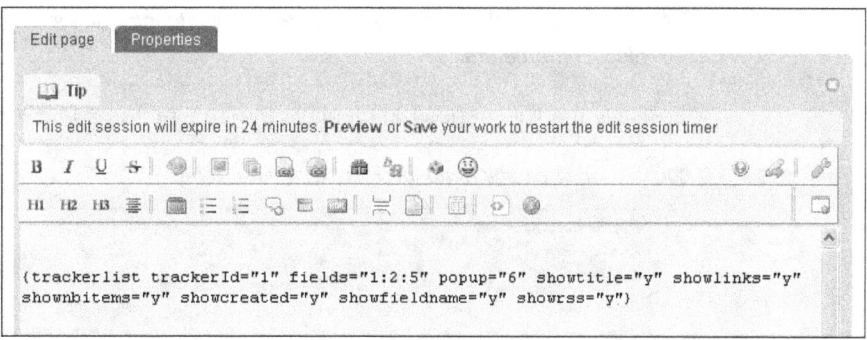

Note   *Be sure to use the tracker field ID and not the order.*

Alternatively, you can use Plugin Help to add the necessary information to the wiki page.

FIGURE 7.79   *Using Plugin Help to add the necessary parameters*

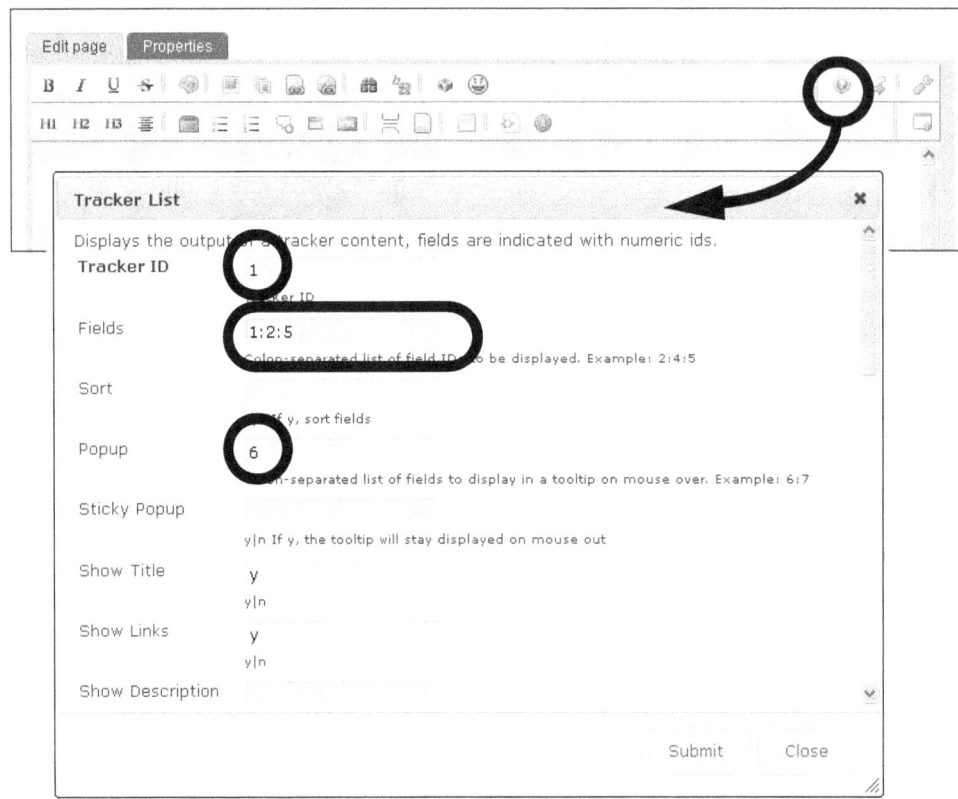

> **Tip**   *See 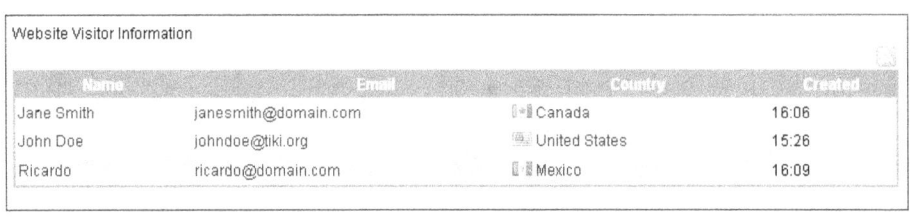 http://doc.tiki.org/Plugin for complete information on the available plugin parameters.*

3. Save the wiki page. Tiki displays the tracker items in a table.

FIGURE 7.80   *Tiki displays the items in the tracker in a table*

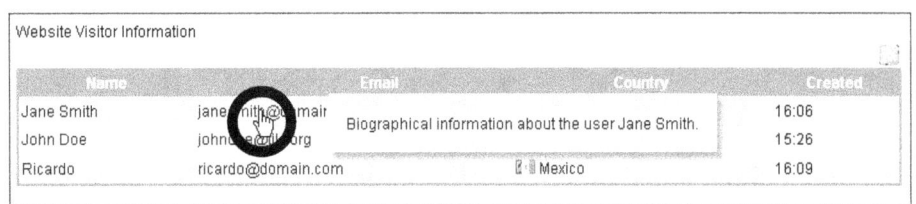

Notice that the **About** information displays in a pop-up window.

Using dynamic lists

A dynamic tracker list is a list field whose options will dynamically change, based on another selection.

For example, we can extend the tracker form we created previously (see "Creating a tracker" on page 77) to allow users to select their operating system: **Windows** or **Solaris**. Depending on their selection, Tiki will automatically display a different list of valid options, depending on which operating system was selected.

Note   *See ⚫ **http://doc.tiki.org/Dynamic+items+list** for more information on dynamic lists.*

To accomplish this, we'll create a separate tracker to maintain the operating system values. We'll refer to this tracker as the "Internal" tracker. We'll refer to the tracker that users will directly interact with as the "External" tracker.

In this section we'll create the "Internal" tracker and then link it to the "External" tracker that you already created.

BUILDING THE "INTERNAL" TRACKER

To create the "Internal" tracker: from which users will select an operating system and (based on the operating system) a version:

1. Create a new tracker. In this example, we'll name the tracker **Operating System**. Because this tracker is used internally, you can leave the options as their defaults.

FIGURE 7.81   *The "internal" tracker*

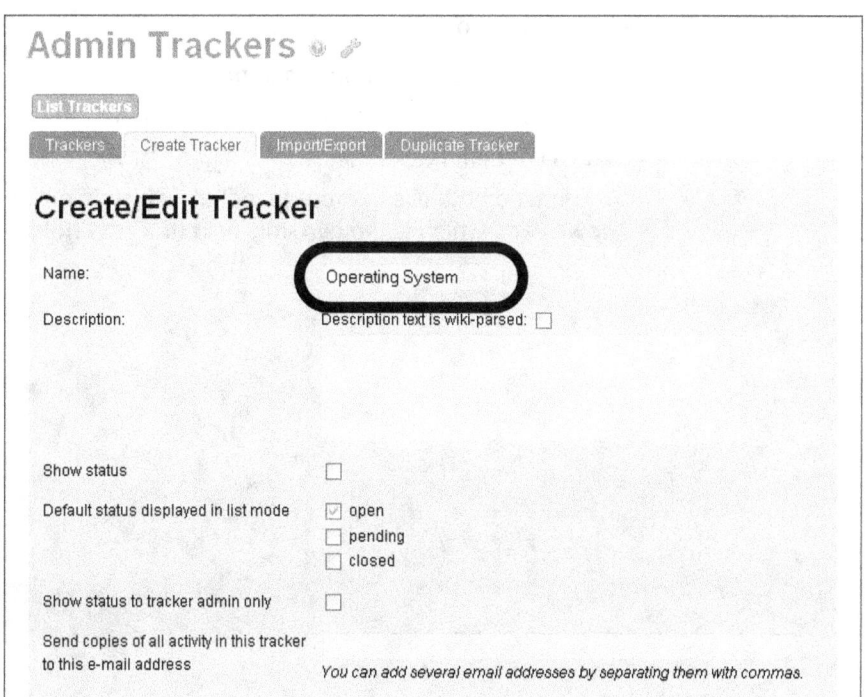

2. Save the "Internal" tracker.

3. Create two fields for the tracker:

TABLE 7.2   *"Internal" tracker fields*

Field	Type	Options
OS	drop down	Windows,Solaris
Version	text field	

Again, you can leave each field's other options as their defaults.

FIGURE 7.82   *"Internal" tracker with two fields*

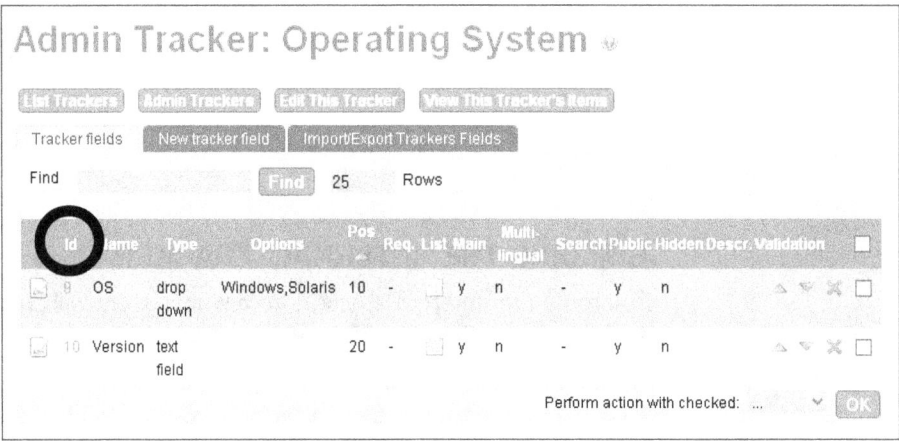

Be sure to record:

- The Tracker ID for this "Internal" tracker

  You'll need this ID in order to add the dynamic list to the "External" tacker.

- The ID of both tracker fields.

  You'll need both IDs in order to identify which is the selection field (the **drop down**) and which is the dynamic field (the **text field**).

POPULATE THE "INTERNAL" TRACKER

Right now, the "Internal" tracker is empty—there are no items from which a user can select their operating system and version. Let's populate the tracker with the necessary options.

1. Using the Tracker interface pages, enter an item for the "Internal" tracker:
   - OS: **Windows**
   - Version: **Vista**

FIGURE 7.83 *Populating the "internal" tracker*

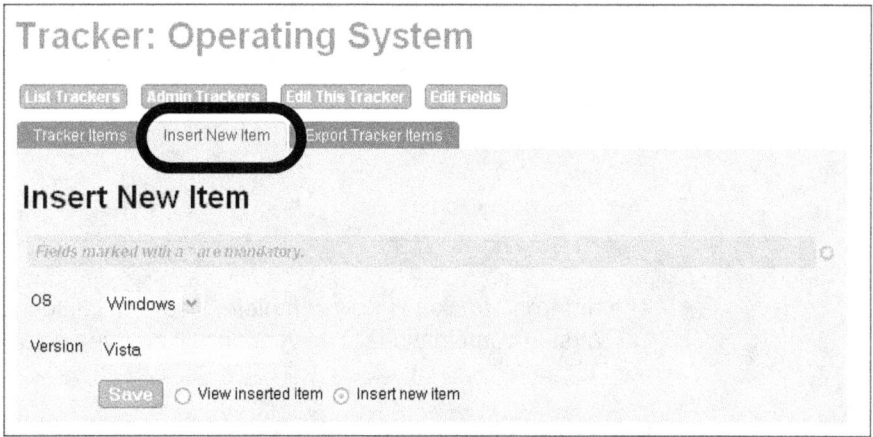

Note *You could create a custom form for entering the operating system options, but in this instance it is easier to use the Tiki Tracker interface.*

This represents one OS/Version combination that users can select.

2. Add additional items to the "Internal" tracker; several for each combination of operating system and version.

TABLE 7.3 *"Internal" tracker items*

Operating System	Version
Windows	XP
Windows	95
Solaris	2.8
Solaris	2.9
Solaris	2.10

3. Your "Internal" tracker should now have six items:

FIGURE 7.84 *The completed internal tracker*

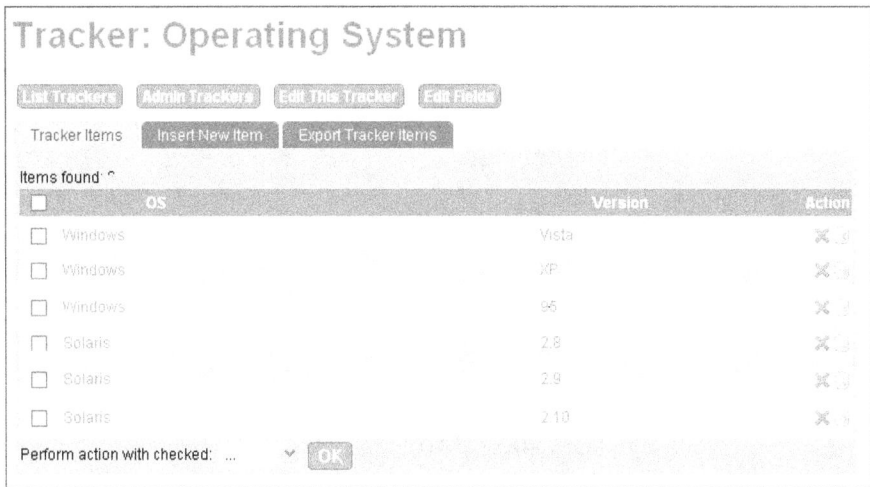

The "Internal" tracker is now complete. Users will select one of these possible OS/Version combinations. The version will be dynamically displayed, based on the OS.

Now let's create the "External" tracker...

BUILDING THE "EXTERNAL" TRACKER

In this section we'll create the "External" tracker—the actual tracker (form) that users will interact with to select their OS and version.

Instead of creating a new tracker, we'll simply use the Website Visitor Information tracker that you created earlier (see "Creating a tracker" on page 77). The Website Visitor Information tracker will be the "External" tracker.

1. Click **Add Field** to add a new field to the tracker.

FIGURE 7.85 *Adding fields to the "External" tracker*

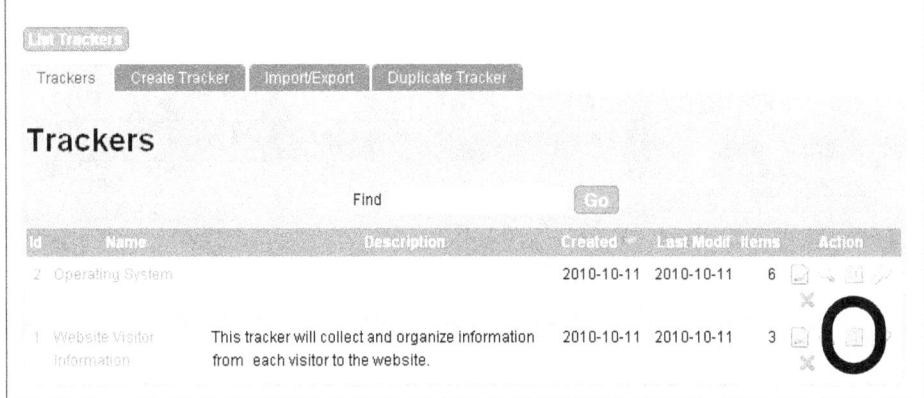

2. Click the **New Tracker Field** tab.

FIGURE 7.86 *External tracker field*

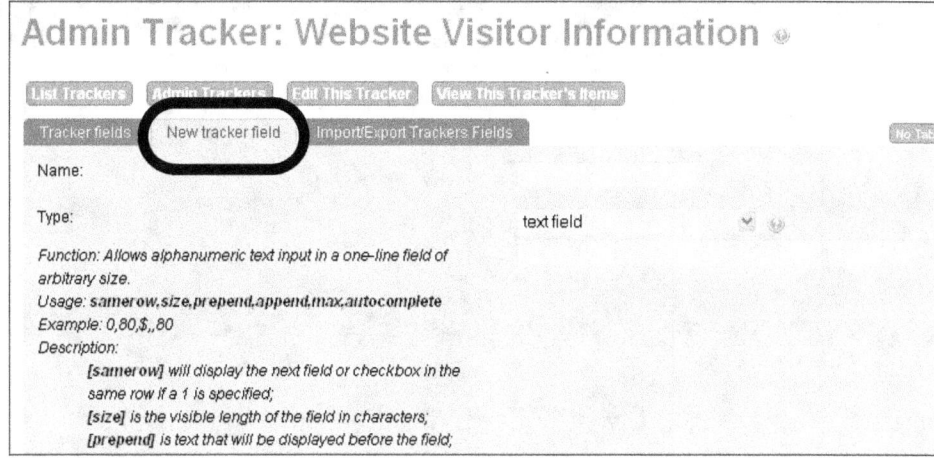

3. Add a new tracker field to the tracker with the following information:
   - **Field**: Operating system
   - **Type**: item link
   - **Options**: *A, B*

   where:
       - **A** = The tracker ID of the "Internal" tracker. See "Building the "internal" tracker" on page 87.
       - **B** = The field ID of the **drop down** field of the "Internal" tracker. See Figure 7.82 on page 88.

4. Add a second tracker field to the tracker with the following information:
   - **Field**: Version
   - **Type**: dynamic items link
   - **Options**: *A, B, C, D*

   where:
       - **A** = The tracker ID of the "internal" tracker. "Building the "internal" tracker" on page 87.
       - **B** = The field ID of the **drop down** field of the "Internal" tracker. See Figure 7.82 on page 88.
       - **C** = The field ID of the **item link** field of the "External" tracker that you created in Step **3**.
       - **D** = The field ID of the **text field** of the "Internal" tracker. See Figure 7.82 on page 88.

Your "External" tracker should appear similar to this:

FIGURE 7.87   *The completed "external" tracker*

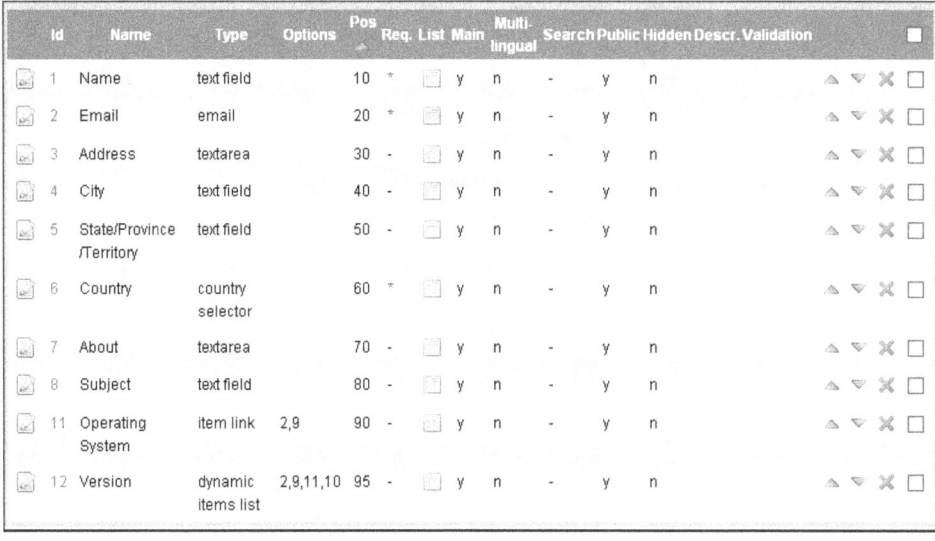

	Id	Name	Type	Options	Pos	Req.	List	Main	Multi-lingual	Search	Public	Hidden	Descr.	Validation				
	1	Name	text field		10	*		y	n	-	y	n				△	▽	✕	☐
	2	Email	email		20	*		y	n	-	y	n				△	▽	✕	☐
	3	Address	textarea		30	-		y	n	-	y	n				△	▽	✕	☐
	4	City	text field		40	-		y	n	-	y	n				△	▽	✕	☐
	5	State/Province /Territory	text field		50	-		y	n	-	y	n				△	▽	✕	☐
	6	Country	country selector		60	*		y	n	-	y	n				△	▽	✕	☐
	7	About	textarea		70	-		y	n	-	y	n				△	▽	✕	☐
	8	Subject	text field		80	-		y	n	-	y	n				△	▽	✕	☐
	11	Operating System	item link	2,9	90	-		y	n	-	y	n				△	▽	✕	☐
	12	Version	dynamic items list	2,9,11,10	95	-		y	n	-	y	n				△	▽	✕	☐

FIGURE 7.88   *The relationship between the "Internal" and "External" trackers*

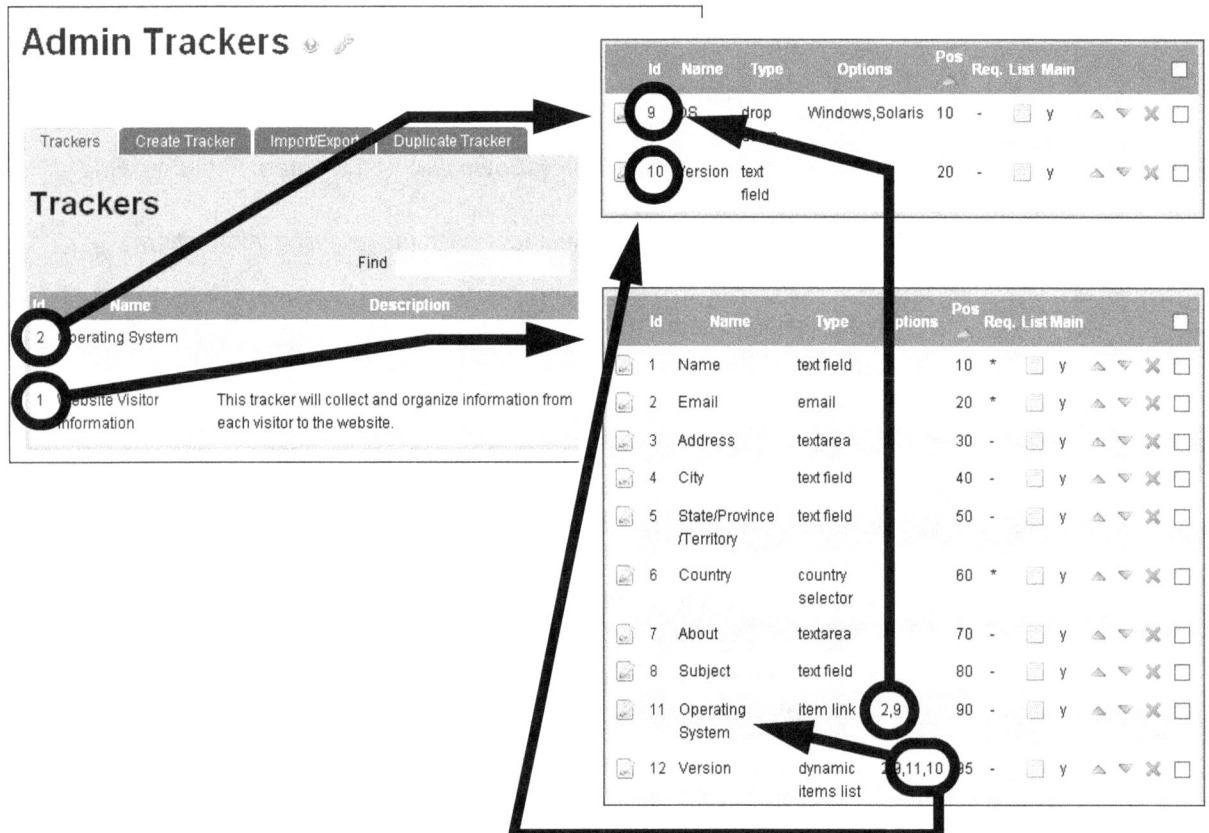

Tiki Essentials

Using the tracker

Now that the "External" tracker includes the dynamic fields, the final step is to update the form we built previously to include these new fields.

1. Update the **Tracker** plugin that you created earlier (see "Entering tracker data" on page 83) to include the two new fields, Operating System and Version, that you added to the "External" tracker (see "Building the "external" tracker" on page 90).

Tracker plugin

```
{TRACKER(trackerId="1", fields="1:2:3:4:5:6:11:12", showtitle="n", showdesc="y",
showmandatory="y", reset="Clear", submit="Send")}Thank you{TRACKER}
```

The form now includes the new fields.

FIGURE 7.89 *The user information form with the new operating system fields*

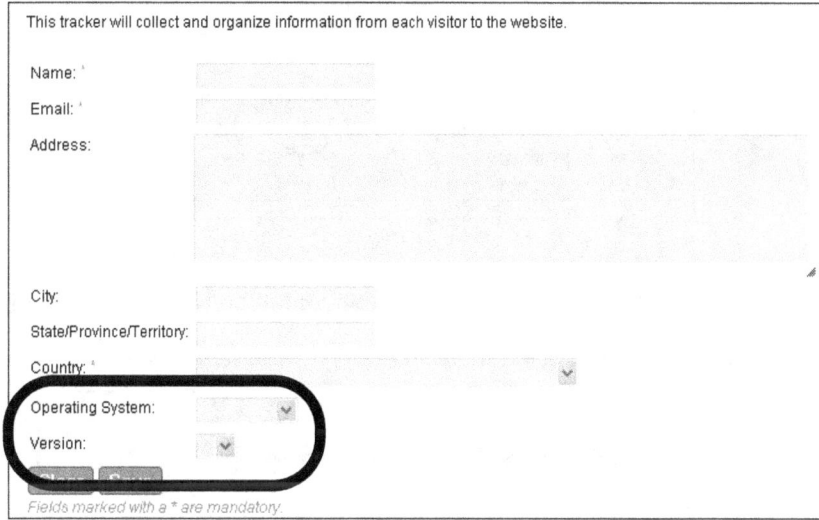

When you select a specific option for the OS, its available version options appear.

2. You should also update the **Trackerlist** plugin (that you created in "Displaying tracker data" on page 85) to display the new fields:

Trackerlist plugin

```
{trackerlist trackerId="1" fields="1:2:6:11:12" popup="7" showtitle="y" showlinks="y"
showcreated="y" showfieldname="y" showrss="y" shownitems="y"}
```

The table now includes the new fields.

FIGURE 7.90 *The user list with the new operating system fields*

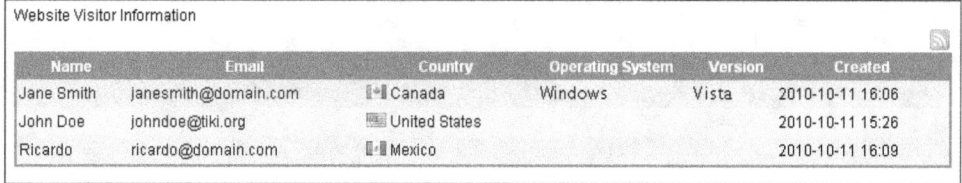

Creating pretty trackers

Normally, when displaying tracker information, with the **Trackerlist** plugin, Tiki displays the information as a table. For example, when building forms, you displayed the tracker data in a table.

With pretty trackers, Tiki can use a predefined Wiki page or Smarty template (TPL) file to display the tracker data. This gives you complete flexibility in presenting the data.

Tip   *Refer to the* 🌐 ***http://doc.tiki.org/Pretty+Tracker*** *for complete information on using pretty trackers.*

For example, instead of displaying the tracker as a table:

FIGURE 7.91   *Displaying tracker items in a table*

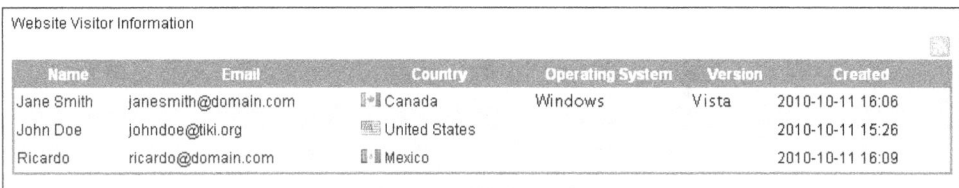

you can display each tracker item on a formatted wiki page:

FIGURE 7.92   *Displaying tracker items in a pretty tracker template*

Building a Pretty Tracker requires:

- creating a tracker (no different from creating any other tracker)
- building a template
- displaying the pretty tracker

Let's update the tracker you've built to use a pretty tracker for display...

BUILDING A TEMPLATE

To display the pretty tracker, you can create a wiki page to serve as the template. You can include any wiki formatting, import graphics and icons, and even include other plugins and modules in this template.

To include the data from a tracker field in the template, including the following code in the wiki page:

{$f_**XX**}

where:

- **XX** = ID of the specific tracker field

For example, to display the user's name, you would use **{$f_1}**.

FIGURE 7.93   *The ID of the **Name** field*

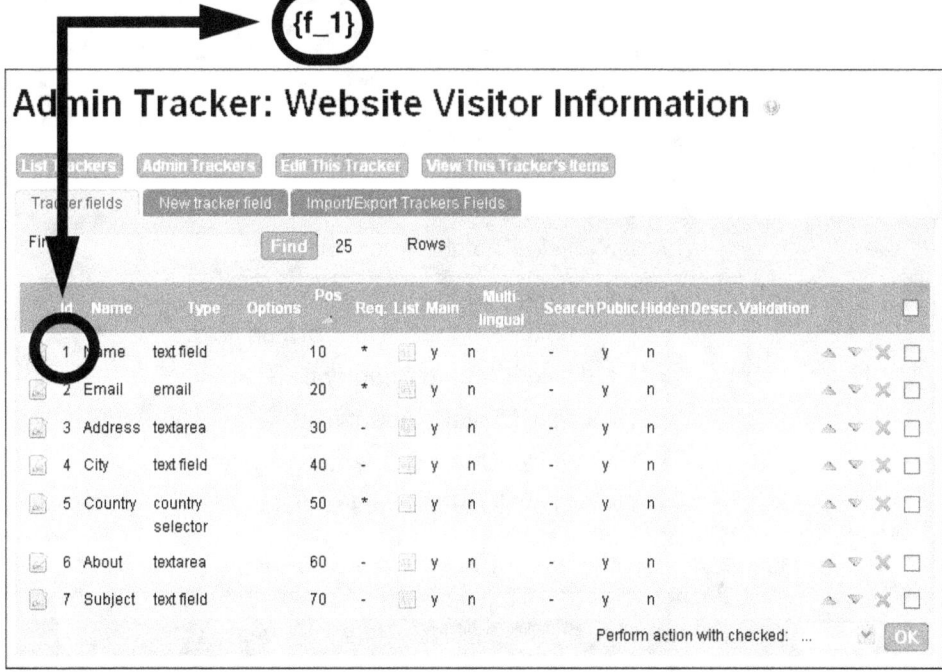

Create the template

The "template" for the pretty tracker is simply a wiki page.

1. Create a new wiki page.
2. In the wiki page, add the following code:

Pretty tracker template

```
{DIV(float=left,width="75px")}{img src="pics/large/users48x48.png"
alt="{$f_1}" desc="{$f_1}"}{DIV}
__{$f_1}__ from {$f_6} uses {$f_11} {$f_12}.
A little about {$f_1}... {$f_8}
{DIV(class="clearfix") /}

For more information, contact {$f_1}:
*Email: [{$f_2}]
*Postal:
+{$f_3}
+{$f_4}, {$f_5} {$f_6}
```

where:

- f_1 = field ID of the Name field.
- f_2 = field ID of the Email field.
- f_3 = field ID of the Address field.
- f_4 = field ID of the City field.
- f_5 = field ID of the State/Province field.
- f_6 = field ID of the Country field.
- f_8 = field ID of the About field.
- f_11 = field ID of the Operating System field.
- f_12 = field ID of the Version field.

FIGURE 7.94 *Wiki page to serve as the template for the pretty tracker*

This will create a template that will display each tracker item as shown in Figure 7.92 on page 94.

3. Save the wiki page. Be sure to record the name of the page—you'll need it in a moment!

DISPLAYING THE PRETTY TRACKER

As before, we'll use the **Trackerlist** plugin to display the pretty tracker. However, there will be some changes to the plugin's parameters.

1. Create a new wiki page.

2. In the wiki page, enter the following:

Trackerlist plugin for pretty tracker

```
{trackerlist trackerId="TRACKER_ID" fields="FIELD:FIELD:FIELD:..."
showtitle="n" showdesc="n" shownbitems="n" showcreated="y"
showfieldname="y" wiki="WIKI_TEMPLATE"}
```

where:

- **TRACKER_ID** = The ID of the tracker that you created.
- **FIELD** = The ID numbers of each tracker field that you created. For this pretty tracker, we'll use all of the fields. If you created a **Subject** field, *do not* include it here.
- **WIKITEMPLATE** = The wiki template page that you created (see "Create the template" on page 96).

3. Save the page. Tiki displays the tracker information, using the wiki page as the template:

FIGURE 7.95 *Using a Pretty Tracker template*

CHAPTER 8

Working with the Tiki MySQL Database

Everything you do in Tiki, from writing wiki pages to changing the site theme, is stored in the MySQL database. There are no "flat" files or configuration files in Tiki. As a result, you can manipulate all of the objects in Tiki (pages, files, and so on) without actually using Tiki; just by working with the database.

This section includes information on how to edit your database to customize your Tiki site, as well as how to access the database from within a Tiki wiki page.

Note *See **http://www.mysql.com** for complete information about MySQL.*

IN THIS CHAPTER

Accessing data from wiki pages

Did you know that you can query your Tiki database (or any other MySQL database) from a wiki page? For example, you can execute a SQL query to count the number of objects in a specific category. This section explains how, by:

- Creating a DSN
- Using the DB Report plugin

CREATING A DSN

In order to access your Tiki data from a wiki page, you must first create a Database Source Name (DSN). This is how Tiki directs your queries to a specific database connection.

Note *See* ***http://doc.tiki.org/Admin+DSN*** *for complete information.*

1. In the **Crosslinks** area at the bottom of the **Administration** page, click **DSN**.

FIGURE 8.96 *Accessing the DSN page*

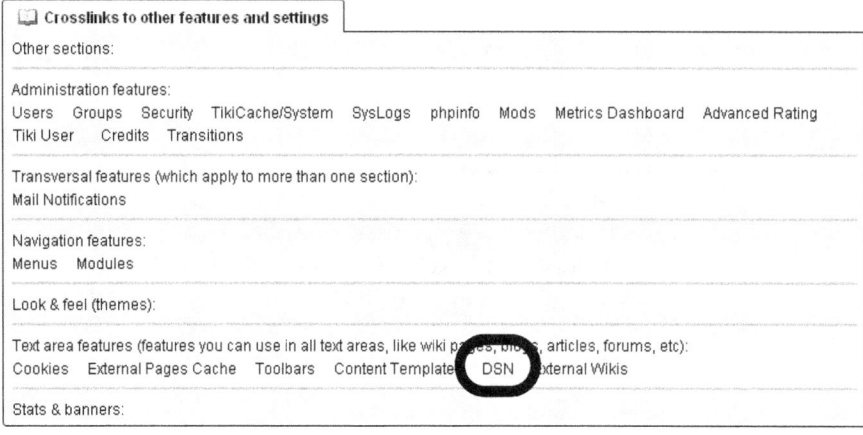

Tiki Essentials

2. On the **Admin: DSN** page, use the **Create/Edit** area to create a new DSN for your Tiki.

FIGURE 8.97 *Creating a new DSN connection.*

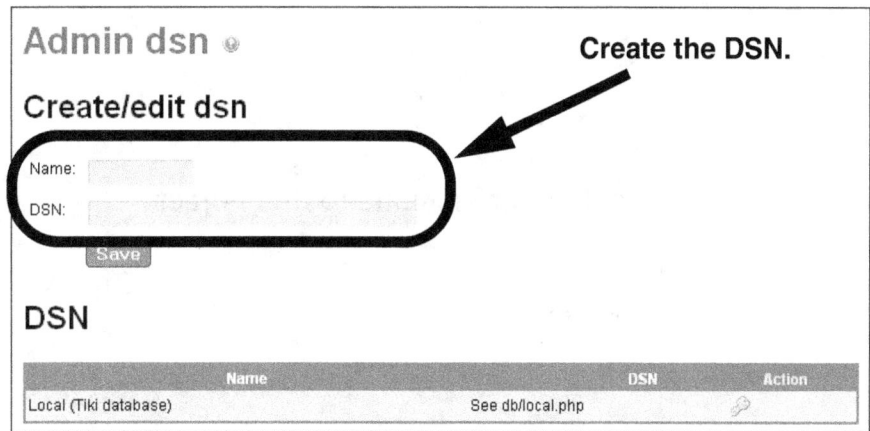

3. Enter the following information in each field:
   - **Name**: The name of the DSN. You will use this name when accessing the database from the wiki page.
   - **DSN**: The database connection information, in the following format:

     `database-type://user:password@host/database-name`

     where:
     - **database-type** = mysql
     - **user** = The database user with access to the database
     - **password** = The password of the database user
     - **database-name** = The name of the database
4. Click **Save**. Tiki adds your new DSN. Now you must specify which of your Tiki groups can use the DSN.
5. Click the **Perms** button 🔑 for the newly created DSN.

FIGURE 8.98 *The available DSN connections*

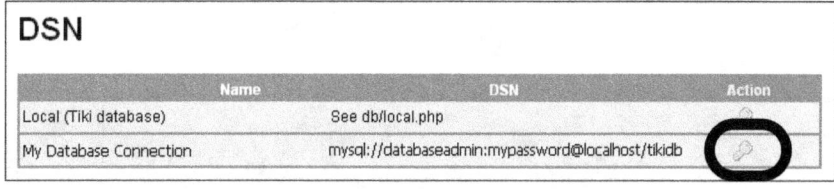

Note *By default, Tiki includes a DSN connection for your local Tiki database.*

6. On the **Assign permissions to this object** page, select which groups should be able to execute queries on the DSN, and click **Assign**.

FIGURE 8.99   *Assigning permissions to the DSN*

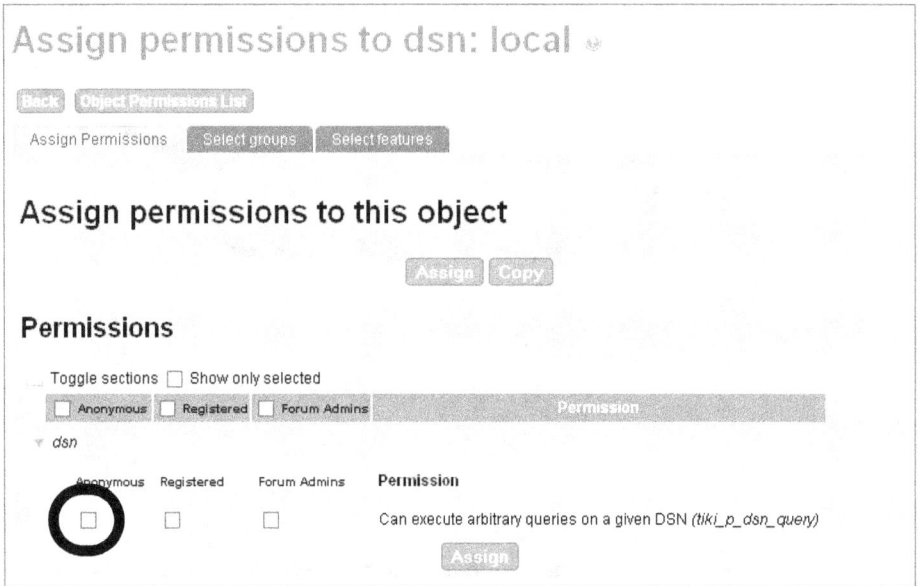

If you want all visitors to have access to the queries on this connection, select the **Anonymous** group.

Warning   *Normally, you should not allow Anonymous users to access the DSN. This can be potentially dangerous and is shown here for demonstration purposes only.*

Now that your DSN is fully configured, you can use the **DB Report** plugin to execute queries against the database. See "Using the DB Report plugin" on page 103.

USING THE DB REPORT PLUGIN

Now that you have a connection (DSN) defined, you can use the **DB Report** plugin to query to access the database and return information to the wiki page.

Note See 🔷 *http://doc.tiki.org/PluginDBReport* for complete information, including options to format the results.

Warning *Using the DB Report and DSN plugins present a potential security hazard, as your are allowing users to directly access the database. You should lock the page to avoid allowing users to see the page source (which would also expose the SQL code).*

Use the DB Report plugin to query the database

You can use the **DB Report** plugin to execute an query against the database.

Sample SQL plugin

```
{DBREPORT(dsn=>"DSN_NAME'')}
    . . .
{DBREPORT}
```

For example, to execute a query that will display the number of objects in a specific Tiki category, you might use:

Finding the number of objects in category #5

```
{DBREPORT(dsn="DSN_NAME")}
    SELECT count(*) FROM `tiki_category_objects` WHERE `categId`=5
{DBREPORT}
```

Updating Tiki preferences

Like almost everything else, your Tiki site preferences (such as which features you have enabled and the configuration settings for each feature) are stored in the database. You can configure all preferences simply by accessing the database.

Tip *This is especially helpful if your site ever "crashes" or you find yourself "locked out" of your site.*

By editing the database tables, you can:

- change preferences
- fix modules
- edit custom code

CHANGING PREFERENCES

The settings and preferences that control your Tiki site are defined in the **tiki_preferences** table in the database.

FIGURE 8.100 *The **tiki_preferences** table*

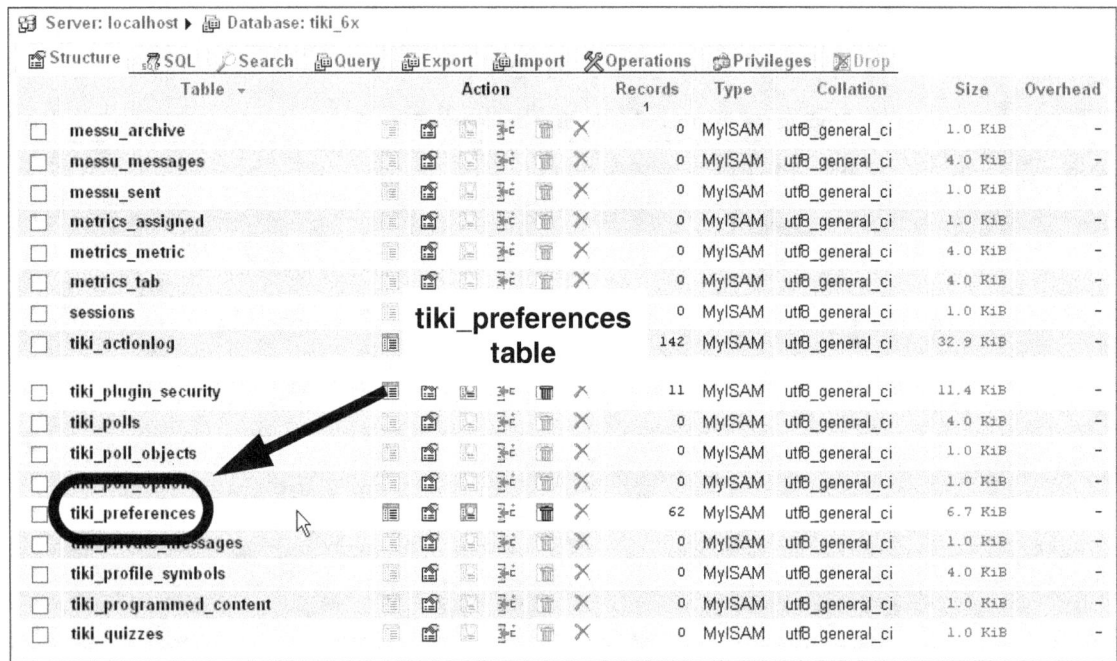

By simply changing settings from **y** to **n** or from **enabled** to **disabled**, you can usually undo any inadvertent damage and regain control of your site.

For example, if you accidentally enable the **Require secure (https) login** option on a site without SSL, you'll find yourself unable to log in (even as the Admin), since Tiki would be looking for a non-existent HTTPS port.

To "reset" the HTTPS option to **disabled** you can edit the **https_login** row in the **tiki_preferences** table:

FIGURE 8.101 *The relationship between the Tiki option and the database field*

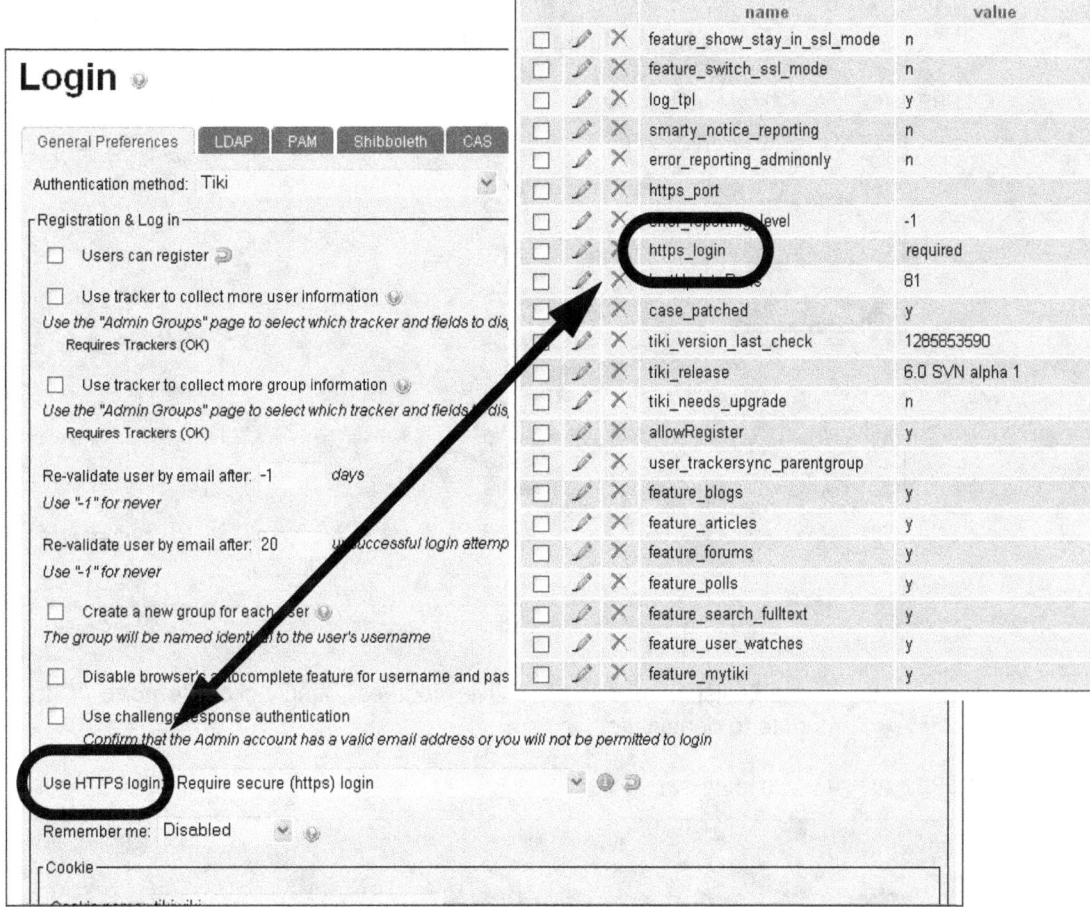

In this example, you would change the field to **disabled** in order to "turn off" the **Use HTTPS login** option.

Other common options, that if inappropriately enabled, could "lock" your Tiki, include:

- authentication method (auth_method)
- SSL options
- inter-Tiki options
- invalid syntax in custom code
- invalid syntax in user modules

FIXING MODULES

When you create a custom user module (see "Using modules" on page 50), Tiki allows you to include custom code, including PHP and Smarty syntax. In some instances, if you add invalid code (such as an improperly formed Smarty expression) your Tiki may display a blank screen.

In this case, you can edit your database (as explained previously) to temporarily deactivate the offending module. This will allow you to access your Tiki and edit or correct the code in the module.

1. Access the **tiki_modules** table of the database.

FIGURE 8.102   *The **tiki_modules** table*

2. The table lists the currently active modules. Simply click **Remove** ✕ for the module to deactivate.

FIGURE 8.103   *Deactivating a module*

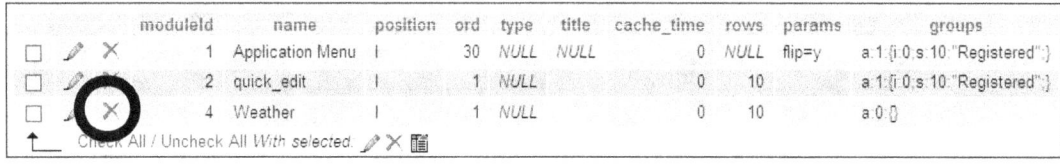

Tip   *This does not delete the module—Tiki simply deactivates it.*

3. Reload your Tiki website.
4. On the **Admin: Modules** page, edit the user module to correct the module's custom code.

EDITING CUSTOM CODE

The **Admin: Look and Feel** page includes several areas in which you can add custom code, including PHP and Smarty syntax. In some instances, if you add invalid code (such as an improperly formed Smarty expression) your Tiki may display a blank screen.

In this case, you can edit your database (see "Updating Tiki preferences" on page 104) to remove or correct the offending code. The following table identifies the appropriate database field in the **tiki_preferences** table for each custom code area on the **Look and Feel** page:

TABLE 8.4 *Custom code areas*

Look and Feel field	tiki_preferences field
Custom HTML Content	feature_custom_html_head_content
Secondary site menu custom code	feature_secondary_sitemenu_custom_code
Custom Site Header	sitemycode
Top Bar, Custom code	feature_topbar_custom_code
Custom Center Column Header	feature_custom_center_column_header
Custom Site Footer	bot_logo_code
Custom End of Code	feature_endbody_code

CHAPTER 9

Joining the Tiki Community

The Tiki Community consists of all the developers, consultants, and end-users (just like you!). By joining the community, you help Tiki to grow. Not only will you be able to find answers to your questions, but you can even become an integral member of the community (if you desire) and help chart the course for Tiki in the future.

FIGURE 9.104 *The Tiki community site*

IN THIS CHAPTER

About the Tiki websites

The Tiki community actively *dogfoods* the Tiki software. This means we **use** Tiki to **develop** Tiki. All of the Tiki websites (collectively referred to as ***.t.o**) are continually updated from the development repository. As a result, some things may not always work or display properly (as the developers continue to add new features and fix existing code).

You can see how "up-to-date" a particular ***.t.o** site is, by reviewing the footer information on each page.

FIGURE 9.105   *Footer information on a t.o site*

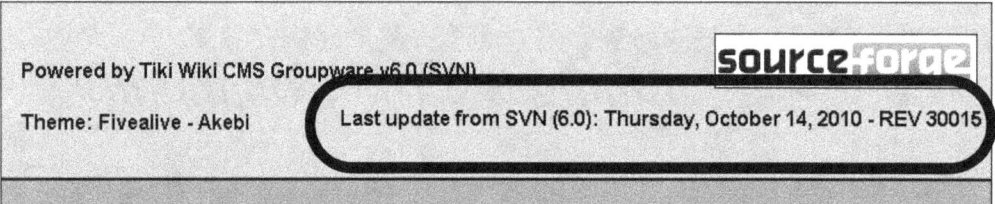

Connecting to the Tiki directory

One way both to promote your site, and to connect with the Tiki Community, is to submit your site to the Tiki directory.

1. From the **Administration** page click **Connect** .
2. On the **Admin: Connect** page, click **Submit Site** to add your site to the Tiki Directory.

FIGURE 9.106   *Getting listed in the Tiki directory*

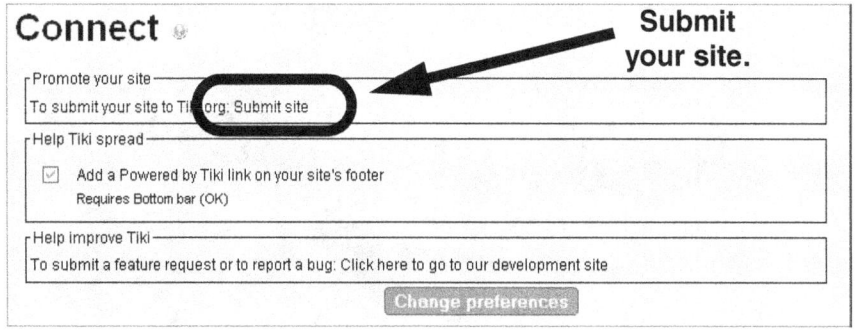

Tip   *You can also use the **Admin: Connect** page to submit a bug report or feature request to the Tiki Developer site, or to add a **Powered by Tiki** link at the bottom of your site.*

3. Use the **Register this Site** page to add your site to the Tiki directory.

FIGURE 9.107 *Register your site*

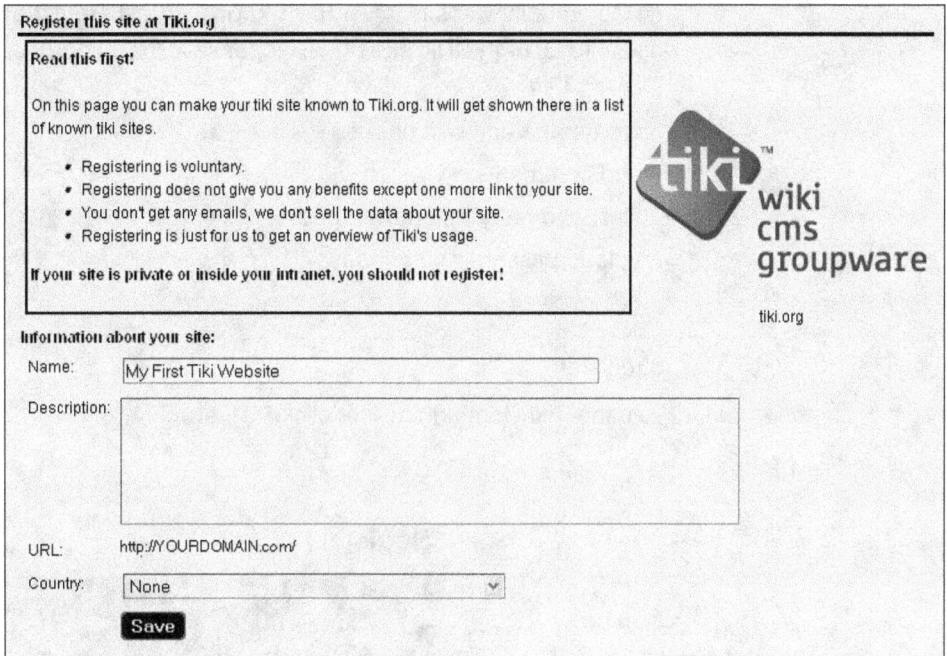

4. Complete the following fields on the page:
   - **Name**: name of your Tiki website
   - **Description**: short description of what your site is about
   - **URL**: URL of your website
   - **Country**: location or language of your site

   Tiki will automatically populate some fields (such as Name and URL) from your site's configuration.

5. Click **Save**. Tiki adds your site's listing to the community directory.

FIGURE 9.108 *Tiki Community directory*

Registering at Tiki.org

The first step in becoming a member of the Tiki community is to register at the Tiki Community website 🌐 **http://tiki.org/Home**. Registration here gives you access to all of the Tiki sites (Developer's Corner, Themes, Profiles, and so on). You'll be able to:

- create and edit wiki pages.
- add comments.
- start and reply to forum threads.
- upload pictures and images.
- get involved.

To register:

1. From the Tiki Community site, click **Register**.

FIGURE 9.109 *Tiki Community site*

You can also use the **Join Tiki** link at the bottom of any ***.t.o** page.

FIGURE 9.110 *Using the Join Tiki link*

2. Complete all the fields on the registration form, and click register.

FIGURE 9.111   *The Registration page*

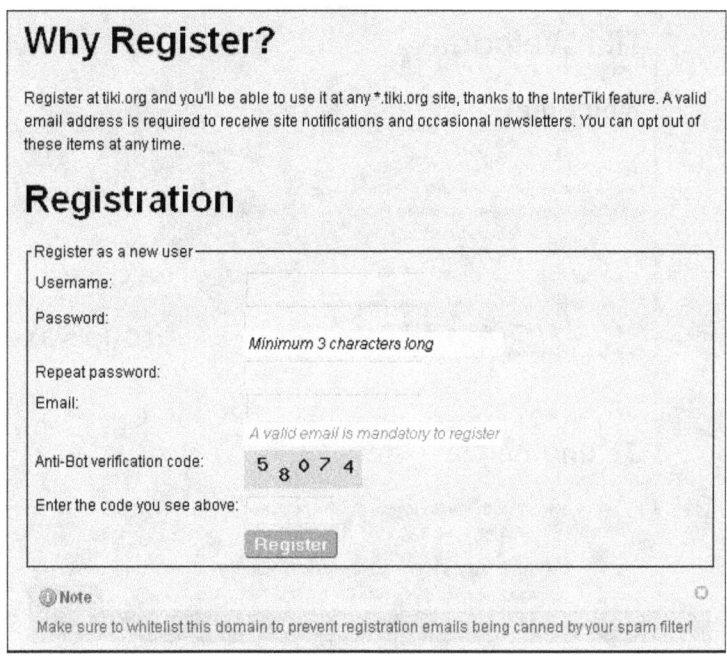

Note   *If you use an email filter, be sure to add the domain **tiki.org** to your "accepted" list.*

In a few moments, you'll receive an email from Tiki:

FIGURE 9.112   *Registration letter*

Hi YOUR USERNAME,

You or someone registered this email address at tiki.org

If you want to be a registered user in this site you will have to use the following link to login for the first time:

http://tiki.org/tiki-login_validate.php?user=USERNAME&pass=0bce23a02992df40574b

Enjoy the site!

3. Click the link.

Make sure that your email client does not "break" the link—it may be quite long.

Tiki automatically validates your registration and the **Tiki Welcome** page appears.

FIGURE 9.113 *The Welcome page*

Tiki Welcome

Welcome!

Welcome to Tiki Wiki CMS Groupware!
Thanks for joining our community. We are
one of the largest open-source teams in
the world , and we're glad that you're part
of the team!

To learn what you can expect from Tiki (and
what we expect from you, as a community
member), please read our Social Contract.

Getting help

Tiki is **very** powerful and includes more out-of-the-box features then any other application (that we're
aware of!). If you need help:

- The first place to look is the official Tiki documentation (http://doc.tiki.org ☑),
  especially the FAQs (http://doc.tiki.org/tiki-list_faqs.php ☑).
- If you're still having problems, you can post a question to the forum (http://tiki.org/tiki-
  forums.php ☑) or ask in our IRC channel: http://irc.tiki.org/ ☑
- There are also several mailing lists (hosted by SourceForge.net) that you can
  subscribe to: http://sourceforge.net/projects/tikiwiki/support ☑

Account information

Your registration gives you access to the other **tiki.org** sites. With one username/password, you can
the Development site, Themes site, Documentation site, and much more.

To update your account information (such as your password and email address, or to
upload an avatar), select **MyTiki > MyTikiHome** from the main Menu.

If you ever forget your password, just visit http://tiki.org/tiki-remind_password.php ☑ to reset your
account.

Getting involved

Now that you're a registered member of the Tiki community, you can help:

- To help with documentation, visit ✉ http://doc.tiki.org.
- To help with development, visit ✎ http://dev.tiki.org.
- To learn about new releases and Tiki news, subscribe to the RSS feed ☐ http://info.tiki.org/tiki-
  articles_rss.php?ver=2.
  Or subscribe via email:

Tiki is also active on many social networks such as Twitter ☑ and Facebook ☑ . See http://tiki.org
/networks ☑ to follow Tiki and become a fan!

Thanks again, and welcome!

Be sure to take a moment to read the welcome letter. It includes a lot of useful information, such as:

- how to get help
- whom to contact for information
- how to become involved

That's it! You're now a member of the Tiki Community.

SOCIAL NETWORKING

Now that you've joined the Tiki Community, you can show your support and interest by joining the Tiki groups on the major social networking sites:

- Facebook
- Twitter
- Ohloh
- and more!

For a complete list of Tiki groups, see **http://tiki.org/Networks**.

Getting help

Tiki is a user-based community with multiple ways to obtain free assistance.

Note   *You can also hire consultants to help with your Tiki site.*
See **http://tiki.org/Consultants** *for more information.*

Don't forget Tiki's internal help system. To access the appropriate documentation, simply click the **Help** button   available on most Admin pages.

FIGURE 9.114   *Tiki help system*

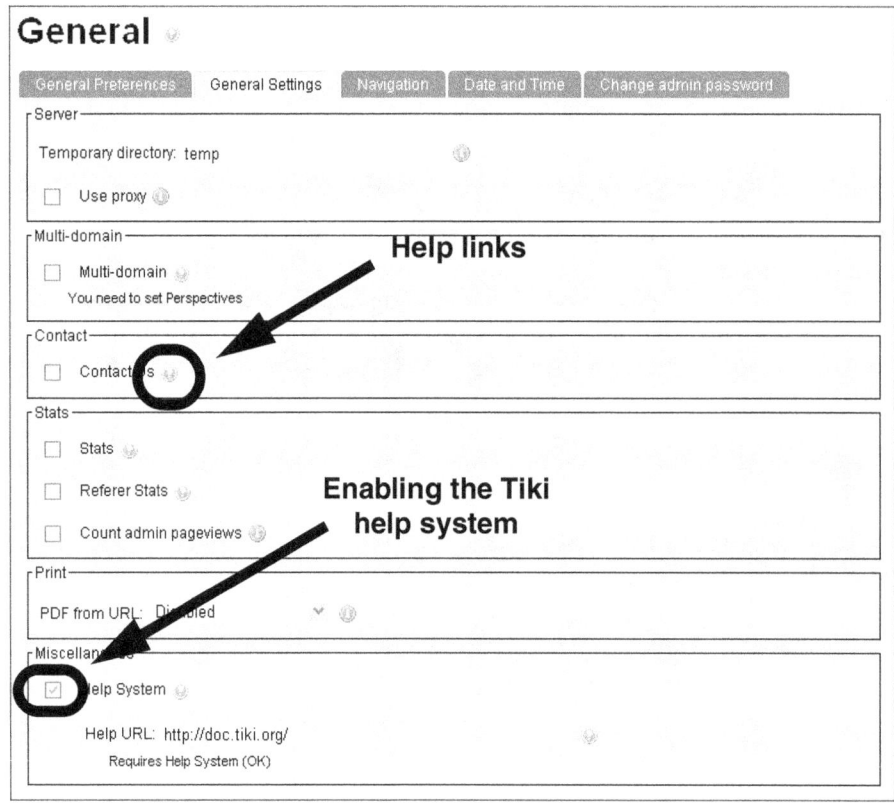

Other ways to get help include:

- using the forums
- chatting on IRC
- subscribing to mailing lists

USING THE FORUMS

The Tiki support forums are maintained on the Tiki Community site. They are fully searchable, and contain posts going back several years. You should use the forums as your primary means of support.

Note   *See*  *http://tiki.org/Forums for more information.*

When posting questions in the forum, keep the following in mind:

- With a six-month release cycle, there may be several different versions of Tiki "in the field" at any time. Be sure to specify exactly the Tiki version you're using. You can find your version on the **Admin: General** page of your site.

- Include as many specifics as possible, such as your PHP and MySQL versions, operating system details, host, and so on.

- When possible, include a URL or image that illustrates the problem.

- Write clearly. The Tiki community is international. Although most information is conveyed in English, not everyone is a native speaker. There are also several language specific forums and Tiki sites.

Accessing the forums

To access the Tiki support forums:

1. From the Tiki Community website select **Support > Forums**.

FIGURE 9.115 *Accessing the support forum*

2. Select the forum that is most appropriate for your question.

FIGURE 9.116 *A partial listing of the Tiki support forums*

3. Simply click the title of the forum to access.

Forum categories

The Tiki Community site contains several different forum categories. Make sure that you post your question in the appropriate category (and please don't cross-post the same question to multiple forums).

- Community and *.tiki.org site organization
- Tiki development
- Tiki support
- Non-English
  - Català
  - Deutsch
  - Español
  - Français
  - Italiano
  - Português

CHATTING ON IRC

One of the primary methods by which Tiki developers communicate with one another is IRC (Internet Relay Chat). **#tikiwiki** is an IRC channel dedicated to Tiki on the **freenode** network. There are usually 15-30 users and developers online at any given time.

If you're unfamiliar with IRC, see 🌐 **http://tiki.org/ConnectingToIrc** for information on how to connect and chat. The Tiki channel is very friendly and everyone online is willing to help.

Some general rules to remember:

- *Don't* "ask to ask"—simply ask your question. If someone can help, they will.
- *Do* check the documentation, FAQs, and forums first. Most questions have already been asked (and answered).
- *Don't* post large amounts of code to the channel. Instead, use a site such as **http://pastebin.com/**.
- *Do* be patient if no one answers immediately. You can always check the chat log later to see if someone offered a suggestion.

    Remember, the world is a big place. That it's 3:00 p.m. for you, doesn't mean the rest of the world is awake, too.

Reviewing the log

Tiki maintains a log of the **#tikiwiki** channel 🌐 **http://irc.tiki.org**. This is especially helpful when checking to see if your question was answered.

FIGURE 9.117   *Reviewing the IRC chat log*

Select a date to review its log

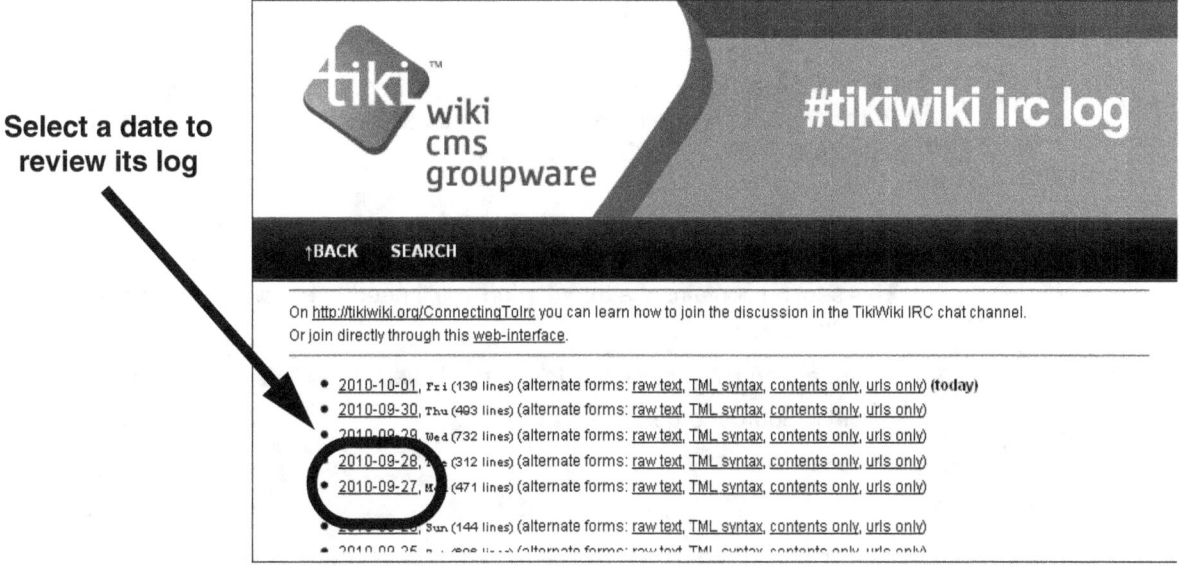

You can "page" through the log, from day-to-day, and perform keyword searches.

MAILING LISTS

In addition to the support forums, the Tiki community maintains several mailing lists for discussion and communication. These mailing lists are hosted by SourceForge.net and include full, searchable archives:

- **tikiwiki-artwork**: All about the Tiki look and feel, graphics, icons, themes, logos, and other GUI stuff
- **tikiwiki-cvs**: SVN commits information, and comments about commits
- **tikiwiki-devel**: Tiki developers (the main decision/communication channel)
- **tikiwiki-pt-br**: Lista de discussão Tiki em português, para usuários e desenvolvedores
- **tikiwiki-users**: General list for Tiki users

See **http://tiki.org/Mailing+Lists** for more information.

Contributing to Tiki

There are different ways to contribute to the Tiki Community and advance the Tiki project. As a developer, you can contribute code, user interface improvements, and other items directly to the code repository. You can also help to keep the Tiki documentation up-to-date, participate in the online forums and chats, and log bugs and feature requests.

No matter how you choose to contribute, you'll find the Tiki community very open and inviting—and fun. If you've never participated in open source development before, here's your chance!

GETTING COMMITTED

Getting committer access to the Tiki Subversion (SVN) repository, hosted on SourceForge.net, allows you to contribute directly to Tiki code development. Becoming a code committer is quick and easy, and allows you to directly affect the future of Tiki Wiki CMS Groupware.

Note *See **http://dev.tiki.org** for details on becoming a Tiki developer.*

This section contains the information you'll need to become a Tiki developer, such as:

- understand, and agree to, the Three Rules
- get a SourceForge account
- ask for access

Understand and agree to the Three Rules

Tiki uses a "wiki way" software development model. With over 200 active developers continuously committing code to the repository, it is important to make the process as easy as possible. While the Tiki development process may seem chaotic and unruly to an outsider, it is important to remember that it has been working well since 2002!

There are really only three rules for contributing code to the Tiki project.

The Three Rules

1. Respect the environment.
2. Commit early, commit often.
3. Make it optional.

All Tiki developers abide by these rules. You'll need to agree too, in order to contribute your code.

Note   *See* **http://dev.tiki.org/3rules** *for details on The Three Rules.*

See **http://tiki.org/Model** *for details on Tiki's "wiki way" model of development.*

Get a SourceForge account

The Tiki SVN code repository is hosted by SourceForge.net – you'll need to have a SourceForg.net account. SourceForge.net registration is free and requires only a valid email address.

Note   *See* **http://www.sourceforge.net** *for details.*

All of your code contributions will be identified by your SourceForge.net username. You can use the same username that you have on the Tiki websites.

Other Accounts

In addition to your SourceForge.net account, you'll also need a Tiki Community account. This will allow you to participate on the Tiki Community websites. See "Registering at Tiki.org" on page 112 for details.

To stay involved with the Tiki community, you should also:

- Subscribe to the Tiki mailing lists, especially the developer's list and SVN commit list. See "Mailing lists" on page 120.
- Subscribe to the Tiki News RSS feed. See **http://tiki.org** for details.
- Join the other Tiki social networking sites such as Twitter, Facebook, and LinkedIn. See "Social networking" on page 115.

Ask for access

Getting commit access to the Tiki SVN repository is as simple as asking for it:

1. Go to the Tiki IRC channel: **#tikiwiki**. See "Chatting on IRC" on page 119.
2. Ask for a Tiki Admin and simply request access to the SVN repository.

One of the Tiki Admins will begin **The Ceremony**:

- You'll need to provide your SourceForge.net account name to the Tiki Admin.
- You'll be asked to read the Three Rules and signify your acceptance.
- The Tiki Admin will add you to the SourceForge.net Tiki project list.

You're now a Tiki Developer!

Welcome to the Tiki Community!

3. You should now set up your local development environment.

Note *It may take several hours for your permission to be updated throughout the servers. In the meantime, you should review the following items on the Tiki Developer site:*

http://dev.tiki.org/DevTips

http://dev.tiki.org/SVNTips

SHARING WHAT YOU KNOW

In addition to contributing code, there are other ways to contribute to the Tiki community—even if you're not a code developer.

- Help on the Tiki forums.

  Remember, everyone was a newbie at one time. There's a good chance that other people have the same questions that you once asked. See "Using the forums" on page 117.

- Join a Tiki Team.

  There are lots of opportunities to help out in marketing, graphics, user interface, translation, and much more. See **http://tiki.org/Teams**.

- Help update the Tiki Documentation. See **http://doc.tiki.org**.

- Become a Tiki Facebook fan and join the other social networks and follow the Tiki on Twitter. See "Social networking" on page 115.

- Attend a TikiFest. See **http://tiki.org/TikiFest**.

- Translate Tiki into your native language. Tiki already contains translations for over 40 languages—add or improve yours! See **http://tiki.org/i18n**.

There are lots of "unofficial" was to help, too.

- Write a review of Tiki for your blog or website.
- Create your own Tiki online reference or guide.
- Help to maintain Tiki-related articles on Wikipedia, WikiHow, and other sites.

Epilogue

While this may be the end of this book, this is most definitely *not* the end of your Tiki journey. This guide has covered only a handful of Tiki's features.

I encourage you to explore the complete Tiki documentation for information on all of Tiki's features, and to join the Tiki Community.

Finally, I am curious about what you think about this guide and the related site: **http://twessentials.keycontent.org**. Any feedback, compliments, or criticism is greatly appreciated. Even better: Become a contributor to the online version of *Tiki Essentials* to help improve future versions of the guide.

Thank you!

Index

www.ingramcontent.com/pod-product-compliance
Lightning Source LLC
Chambersburg PA
CBHW081152180526

45170CB00006B/2039